What Does the Bible Say About Homosexuality?

David Stewart

Stewart Publications
Searcy, Arkansas
www.stewartpublications.net

ISBN: 0-9785917-2-0

CONTENTS

Introduction

Over the course of the past century, public opinion in the United States and many other countries around the world has been radically swayed on the issue of homosexuality.[1] Several of these nations once had sodomy laws which severely punished men who engaged in sexual intercourse with one another. Such acts were kept secret for fear of prosecution or public shame. In just a short time, such laws have been abrogated and social stigmas have been removed. What was once considered repulsive and unmentionable is heralded as an acceptable, alternative way of life.

What changed? It is important to realize that the promotion of homosexual behavior is directly linked to the broader sexual revolution. Wood and Dietrich trace the roots of sexual liberation throughout the late 1800's and 1900's in the United States, showing how influential thinkers, technology, and social conditions shaped modern thought.[2] Atheistic philosophers convinced many people that they were just "human animals" and that sexual desire was simply an animal drive that needed to be fulfilled. Technology produced contraceptives that lessened the responsibility that comes with sexual activity. If those failed, abortion became a viable option. Further, advances in media technology became vehicles for more widely disseminating "free-love" messages and pornography. Changing social conditions such as war, urbanization, industrialization, and declining spirituality were also influential factors.

---

[1]The term "homosexuality" will generally be used to refer to same-sex behavior, whether among men or women. In some places, it will be restricted to same-sex behavior among men in contrast to lesbianism.

[2]Glenn G. Wood and John E. Dietrich, *The AIDS Epidemic: Balancing Compassion and Justice* (Portland, Ore.: Multnomah Press, 1990), 51-81.

The homosexual movement has piggybacked on the sexual revolution. However, activists have had to work more diligently in order to convince society to accept homosexuality as a way of life. This is most likely due to the fact that same-sex acts are contrary to nature. Based on the Kinsey Report (1948), many supporters once propagated the myth that 10% of the male population was homosexual. They reasoned that if such a significant percentage of people engaged in same-sex behavior, then that would legitimize their actions.

In addition, some proponents have tried to convince society that homosexuality has a genetic cause. However, scientific studies have not proven that same-sex desires are inborn. The often cited hypothalamus research done by Simon LeVay (1991) has certainly not been successful to this end. If homosexuality were genetic, then each set of identical twins would be either heterosexual or homosexual—and research has proven that this is not the case.

Activists have also tried to gain status as a minority. Based on their so-called "sexual orientation," they have tried to gain special rights just as women and racial minorities have. However, this is a faulty grouping. One does not choose his/her gender or race, but homosexual activity is a behavioral choice. People are always talking about "the gay and lesbian community." It is interesting that we do not hear much about "the fornicating community," "the adulterous community," "the incestuous community," or "the polygamist community."

The homosexual movement has gained much ground in the political arena. Beyond gaining the abrogation of sodomy laws, homosexual activists have also argued for marriage rights and related benefits—privileges traditionally reserved for a husband and wife. They insist on antidiscrimination when it comes to military service, employment, and housing. In other words, commanding officers, employers, and landlords must tolerate moral depravity; their decisions cannot be based on character. Further, activists promote "diversity" training in major businesses and public schools. Many employees and students are being indoctrinated with the belief that homosexuality is an acceptable, alternative lifestyle. Several large corporations have endorsed the movement, feeding its lobbying groups and other organizations millions of dollars each year. Beyond all this, some religious groups have accepted homosexual behavior among their members—and even their leaders!

Homosexuality was once denounced by every Jewish synagogue and every Christian church as a sin, by psychiatrists as a sickness, and by the law as a crime. What happened? Were our ancestors wrong? Did the truth change? It is time to return to the sacred pages of the Bible and regain our spiritual focus. What does God have to say about the practice of homosexuality?

While some today might mock the idea of being governed by an antiquated book, the Bible has stood the test of time. Just as God has revealed his power and love through creation, he has also disclosed himself through the inspired Word (2 Timothy 3:16-17; 2 Peter 1:20-21). Over the centuries, the Bible has provided guidance for godly living to those willing to submit to its authority. It has a hallowed place in American history, having been used by the framers of the Declaration of Independence and the Constitution.[3] Most politicians still lay their hands on it in reenactment ceremonies after they have been sworn into office. Ultimately, it will be the standard used by Christ to evaluate us on the Day of Judgment (John 12:48).

---

[3]See David Barton, *Original Intent: The Courts, the Constitution, and Religion*, 2nd ed. (Aledo, Tex.: WallBuilder Press, 1997).

1. Deity's Design (Genesis 1-2)

We begin our study of homosexuality by looking at the creation narrative. It is here that we are given a clear, positive view of God's intention for human sexuality. Genesis 1:27-28 records, *So God created man in his own image, in the image of God he created him; male and female he created them. God blessed them and said to them, "Be fruitful and increase in number; fill the earth and subdue it."* The LORD made two genders that are distinguished biologically, emotionally, and socially. He created the two complementary sexes and commanded them to populate the world together.

In Genesis 2, the camera lens zooms in to get a closer look at the sixth day of creation. God had formed the man from dust and breathed into his nostrils the breath of life. He had placed the man in the Garden of Eden to cultivate it and had given him dominion over all the animals. However, there was no one quite like the man with whom he could share intimate companionship. *The LORD God said, "It is not good for the man to be alone. I will make a helper suitable for him"* (Genesis 2:18). After causing the man to fall into a deep sleep, God took a rib from his side and fashioned a woman.

When the man awoke and received his new bride, his heart was overjoyed. *The man said, "This is now bone of my bones and flesh of my flesh; she shall be called 'woman,' for she was taken out of man"* (Genesis 2:23). This first love poem celebrates the fact that there was now someone similar to the man—yet different—with whom he could share his life. The woman and man were alike in the sense that they were both human beings, but they were distinguished by their genders.

The narrator continues the account by explaining that God's complementary design is the foundation for marriage: *For this reason a man will leave his father and mother and be united to his wife, and they will become one flesh* (Genesis 2:24). Since the woman was made from the man, a man would later leave his parents' home and *be united to his wife.* This phrase excludes homosexual pairing, a fact which is emphasized in the Talmud. It repeatedly states, "*. . . and he shall cleave*, but not to a male."[4]

The two would come together in marriage as *one flesh.* This phrase refers to the spiritual and emotional oneness of the couple, as well as sexual intercourse in which the couple's bodies are united together physically (see 1 Corinthians 6:16). In the New Testament, both Jesus and Paul quote Genesis 2:24 as authoritative proof that God created male and female for the marriage relationship (Matthew 19:5; Ephesians 5:31).

The sexual relationship is a gift from God uniquely designed for marriage. The true purpose of sexual relations is at least threefold:

1) Permanence. Sex is designed as a tool for bonding a husband and wife together for life. This begins after the wedding when the marriage is consummated. It allows a husband and wife to "know" each other in a way that nobody else does; it is experiential and personal. The two become one flesh, cleave to each other, and grow together. This continued bonding should not be neglected, except for a short time for the purpose of prayer. If both spouses satisfy each other, then there will be little temptation to look for sexual gratification elsewhere (1 Corinthians 7:3-5).

2) Pleasure. Sex is designed to bring mutual pleasure to a husband and wife. The delight and desire that a groom and a bride share for one another is celebrated in the Song of Songs.

---

[4]Talmud *Sanhedrin* 58a. *Genesis Rabbah* 18.5 rightly says that the phrase excludes his neighbor's wife, a male, or a beast.

Moreover, Proverbs admonishes a man to enjoy the wife of his youth: *A loving doe, a graceful deer—may her breasts satisfy you always, may you ever be captivated by her love* (Proverbs 5:19).[5]

3) Procreation. Sex is also designed for a husband and wife to reproduce children. God gave Adam and Eve this command: "*Be fruitful and increase in number; fill the earth and subdue it*" (Genesis 1:28). The joy of childbirth was first expressed by Eve when she had her firstborn son Cain. She exclaimed, "*With the help of the* LORD *I have brought forth a man*" (Genesis 4:1). Later, after the destruction of the Flood, God repeated his command to Noah: "*Be fruitful and increase in number and fill the earth*" (Genesis 9:1). Over the course of human history, couples have procreated and the earth has been substantially filled as God desired.[6]

At the Fall, sin entered the world and man became corrupt. One significant area in which this corruption is blatantly obvious is man's perversion of God's original intention for marriage and sex. Therefore, both in the Old and New Testaments, heterosexual sex within the covenant of marriage is protected by laws against fornication, adultery, homosexuality, and bestiality. An individual is *not* to have sexual relations outside the covenant of marriage, with another person's spouse, with someone of the same gender, or with an animal. These regulations from God were designed to protect the sacred institution of marriage and the gift of sex (Hebrews 13:4).

---

[5]Some later Jewish writers wrongly opposed the pleasure aspect of sexual intercourse (Josephus *Against Apion* 2.199; Philo *Special Laws* 3.32-36). The very fact that God designed both the husband and wife to be capable of reaching a climax points in the direction of mutual pleasure. If intercourse were simply for procreation, then only the husband would need to climax. Further, sex remains a valuable bonding tool for older couples who are past the age of reproducing.

[6]Some may argue that homosexuality is acceptable now since the world has been substantially filled. Based on this argument, one could also justify other perversions such as bestiality and necrophilia.

If some other sexual/marital configuration were intended by God, the scene of creation in Genesis 1-2 would have looked much differently:

Polygamous:	Adam	& Eve	& Evelyn
Polyandrous:	Eve	& Adam	& Steve
Homosexual:	Adam	& Steve	
Lesbian:	Eve	& Evelyn	
Bisexual:	Adam	& Eve	& Steve

These alternative paradigms are perverted distortions of the true, biblical picture. It is noteworthy that the ancient Greeks invented their own creation stories in order to legitimize the immoral practice of homosexuality.[7] Those who adopt such faulty paradigms do so to their own spiritual, psychological, and physical detriment.

From the very beginning, God intended for one man and one woman to be married for a lifetime. The woman was created from the man's side so that she was a part of him. The two came together and became one flesh. God created sexual relations as a beautiful gift for a husband and wife to share. He intended for them to reproduce children and to provide a stable family in which their children could grow.

---

[7]See Plato *Symposium* 189C-194E. In this text, Aristophanes (satirically?) claims that there were three original beings: a man-woman, a woman, and a man. The Greek god Zeus split each one in half, so that now one half longs for the other. A man and a woman desire one another (heterosexuality), a woman desires a woman (lesbianism), and a man desires a man (homosexuality). Based on this paradigm, he argues that a homosexual was "born to be a lover of boys or the willing mate of a man, eagerly greeting his own kind" (192B). In response to such foolishness, the Jewish philosopher Philo writes, "All these [stories] are seductive enough, calculated by the novelty of the notion to beguile the ear, but the disciples of Moses trained from their earliest years to love the truth regard them with supreme contempt and continue undeceived" (*The Contemplative Life* 63).

2. Noah's Nakedness (Genesis 6-9)

The earliest homosexual acts recorded in the Bible may be found in the narrative about Noah. The author presents some general statements which explain God's rationale for sending the destructive flood waters on the earth: *The LORD saw how great man's wickedness on the earth had become, and that every inclination of the thoughts of his heart was only evil all the time* (Genesis 6:5) and *God saw how corrupt the earth had become, for all the people on earth had corrupted their ways* (Genesis 6:12). While the terms *wickedness*, *evil*, and *corrupt* are generic, it is interesting that some ancient Jews understood these texts to include homosexuality and bestiality.[8]

In addition, there is also a strong emphasis in the flood narrative on mating male and female according to their kind. God promised Noah, "*But I will establish my covenant with you, and you will enter the ark—you and your sons and your wife and your sons' wives with you*" (Genesis 6:18). After the floodwaters subsided, these couples would leave the ark and repopulate the earth (Genesis 7:13; 8:16, 18; 9:1, 18-19; 10:1-32). Furthermore, God commanded Noah, "*You are to bring into the ark two of all living creatures, male and female, to keep them alive with you*" (Genesis 6:19). This action was essential for propagating the various species of birds, animals, and reptiles after leaving the ark (Genesis 6:20; 7:2-3, 14-16; 8:17, 19). While the perverse behavior of Noah's generation led to destruction, the righteous behavior of Noah's family and the animals that entered the ark brought about life.

Unfortunately, the righteousness of Noah's family deteriorated after the Flood. Genesis 9:20-23 explains:

---

[8]Talmud *Sanhedrin* 108a; *Genesis Rabbah* 26.5; 27.3; *Leviticus Rabbah* 23.9; 2 *Enoch* 34.1-3.

Noah, a man of the soil, proceeded to plant a vineyard. When he drank some of its wine, he became drunk and lay uncovered inside his tent. Ham, the father of Canaan, saw his father's nakedness and told his two brothers outside. But Shem and Japheth took a garment and laid it across their shoulders; then they walked in backward and covered their father's nakedness. Their faces were turned the other way so that they would not see their father's nakedness.

There are three plausible interpretations of this story to which we turn our attention:[9]

1) Sodomy. It has been suggested that Ham committed sodomy against his drunken father Noah. The phrase *saw his father's nakedness* could be an idiom referring to sexual intercourse. Throughout Leviticus 18, *uncover the nakedness of* (NASB) refers to *sexual relations.*[10] Moreover, when Noah awoke from his stupor, he *found out what his youngest son had done to him* (Genesis 9:24). In the Ancient Near East, men sometimes sodomized other men in order to assert their dominance over them. They insulted their masculinity by penetrating them like women.

2) Incest. Another possibility is that Ham committed incest with his mother. Again, *saw his father's nakedness* would be an idiom for sexual relations, but Ham's partner would have been Noah's wife. Support for this view comes from the language of Leviticus 18:8 and 20:11 (NASB). The first passage says, "'*You shall not uncover the nakedness of your father's wife; it is your father's nakedness.*'" The second reads, "'*If there is a man who lies with his father's wife, he has uncovered his father's nakedness. . . .*'" Perhaps Ham

---

[9]A fourth explanation is that Ham castrated his father Noah (Talmud *Sanhedrin* 70a), but this interpretation goes far beyond the language of the text.

[10]However, this idiom is always used for heterosexual intercourse.

was seeking to supplant his father's authority by sleeping with his mother (see Genesis 35:22; 49:4; 2 Samuel 16:21-22).

3) Voyeurism. Perhaps Ham simply saw Noah's nakedness and got some perverted pleasure from it. This literal interpretation is the most likely due to repetition in the text. Ham *saw*, but Shem and Japheth *did not see*. Further, the fact that Ham did not cover his father and then broadcast the news to his brothers points to his blatant disrespect. On the other hand, Shem and Japheth walked backward into their father's tent and honorably covered him with a garment. They displayed respect for their parents, an important principle emphasized throughout the Bible (Exodus 20:12; 21:15, 17; Matthew 15:1-9; Romans 1:30; Ephesians 6:1-3).

Ham dishonored his father Noah, who in turn responded with a curse on Ham's son Canaan. While Ham may not have engaged in homosexual intercourse, he at least engaged in shameful mockery and perhaps homosexual lust. Later in Genesis, it is not surprising to discover that Ham's descendants, the Canaanites, were participating in homosexual activity. For this and other perversions, God vomited them out of the land and gave it to his people Israel (Leviticus 18:24-30; 20:22-26).

Shameful mockery and homosexual lust are soundly condemned by the LORD: "*Woe to him who gives drink to his neighbors, pouring it from the wineskin till they are drunk, so that he can gaze on their naked bodies*" (Habakkuk 2:15). Such perverse lust continues today in the forms of homosexual bath houses, sex clubs, peep shows, and pornography.

3. Sulfurous Sodom (Genesis 18-19)

Perhaps the best known story concerning homosexuality in the Old Testament is that of Sodom and Gomorrah. The events of Genesis 19 are foreshadowed in two descriptions found earlier in the narrative. Genesis 13:13 reports, *Now the men of Sodom were wicked and were sinning greatly against the LORD.* Moreover, Genesis 18:20 says, "*The outcry against Sodom and Gomorrah is so great and their sin so grievous.*" These two cities were wicked in the eyes of God and received their just punishment—burning sulfur rained down from heaven and consumed them. Only Abraham's nephew Lot and his two daughters escaped this calamity.

We turn our attention to the central part of the narrative in Genesis 19:1-11:

The two angels arrived at Sodom in the evening, and Lot was sitting in the gateway of the city. When he saw them, he got up to meet them and bowed down with his face to the ground. "My lords," he said, "please turn aside to your servant's house. You can wash your feet and spend the night and then go on your way early in the morning."

"No," they answered, "we will spend the night in the square."

But he insisted so strongly that they did go with him and entered his house. He prepared a meal for them, baking bread without yeast, and they ate. Before they had gone to bed, all the men from every part of the city of Sodom—both young and old—surrounded the house. They called to Lot, "Where are the men who came to you tonight? Bring them out to us so that we can have sex with [know] them."

Lot went outside to meet them and shut the door behind him and said, "No, my friends. Don't do this wicked thing. Look, I have two daughters who have never slept with [known] a man. Let me bring them out to you, and you can do what you like with them. But don't do anything to these men, for they have come under the protection of my roof."

"Get out of our way," they replied. And they said, "This fellow came here as an alien, and now he wants to play the judge! We'll treat you worse than them." They kept bringing pressure on Lot and moved forward to break down the door.

But the men inside reached out and pulled Lot back into the house and shut the door. Then they struck the men who were at the door of the house, young and old, with blindness so that they could not find the door.

For many centuries, this narrative has been understood as a condemnation of homosexual behavior; it is an evil practice that invites the wrath of God. Further, the English term "sodomy," which denotes one male having anal intercourse with another male, is derived from this story about Sodom. To prevent such wicked behavior, many nations around the world had once enacted sodomy laws with severe punishments. Due to secularization and liberalism, several countries have repealed these laws. Unfortunately, there is not much social pressure left to deter a person from committing such lewd acts.

In the last few decades, some homosexual activists have tried to reinterpret Genesis 19 in a desperate effort to support their cause. They have put forth the following explanations:

1) Lot did not have the right of hospitality. Some think Lot did not have the right to offer hospitality to the two strangers since he himself was a foreigner in the city. This argument makes Lot the culprit for taking the two men (angels) into his own home and not allowing the men of Sodom to "know" them. "Know" is interpreted to mean "get acquainted with," "examine," or "interrogate." The Sodomites are portrayed as being suspicious; they did not want just anyone staying in their city.

However, it was Sodom that was destroyed, not Lot! This argument wrongly defends the perverse men of Sodom. These men were *really* saying: "Who are you, Lot, as a foreigner, to offer protection and security to these two men whom we, the native Sodomites, were going to molest at the gate?" Certainly the biblical writer did not desire for his readers to empathize with the doomed inhabitants of the city.

2) The Sodomites were acting inhospitably toward the two men (angels). They were not treating kindly the two men who had come under the protection of Lot's roof. Obviously hospitality is important to the story. Whenever a host welcomed a guest into his home, he became responsible for that person's safety and well-being. The protection of one's guests was so important in the Ancient Near East that Lot was willing to sacrifice the purity of his own daughters for it—an act which is appalling to modern readers!

The men of Sodom were threatening the security of Lot's guests, but there is much more to the story. Their perverseness is emphasized by the drawn out deliberation between the righteous LORD and his servant Abraham over the wicked city's destruction (Genesis 18:16-33). Moreover, terms like *wicked*, *sinning greatly*, and *sin so grievous* do not fit inhospitality (Genesis 13:13; 18:20). Such strong language points to more offensive sins.

3) Sodom's sin is only one of violence (rape). Some suggest that Sodom's sin was its violent behavior, not homosexuality. Therefore, they reason that homosexuality is acceptable in a loving relationship between two consenting adults. However, this interpretation does not take into consideration other factors. While violence and rape are clearly wrong, there is another issue at the heart of Sodom's wickedness: the thought of men "knowing" (*yada'*) men, a clear reference to sodomy.[11]

---

[11]The Hebrew word *yada'* appears 943 times in the Old Testament, but only refers to sexual relations 16 times. In Genesis 19:5, the word "know" obviously refers to homosexual relations (see Judges 19:22). It is interpreted in this way throughout Jewish literature (Philo *On Abraham* 133-141; Josephus *Antiquities* 1.200-201; *Genesis Rabbah* 26.5; 50.5, 7; *Leviticus Rabbah* 23.9; *2 Enoch* 10.4-5).

The Sodomites came at night to "know" the two men and became violent in order to satiate their lust. Instead, Lot offered them his virgin daughters who had not "known" a man. He believed it would be less perverse to give his own daughters to the men of Sodom; at least it would be men "knowing" women. Obviously heterosexual intercourse is more fitting with the created order than homosexual relations—even though this was an abusive situation outside the context of marriage. Lot offered the Sodomites a lesser of two evils in his way of thinking. It is noteworthy that, in the parallel story found in the book of Judges, the manservant is not offered as a substitute; rather, only women are offered (Judges 19:19, 24).[12]

In the end, God destroyed Sodom and Gomorrah with burning sulfur, punishing them for their perversion. In the rest of Scripture, Sodom and Gomorrah are used as a symbol of wickedness and destruction (Isaiah 1:9-10; 13:19; Jeremiah 23:14; 49:18; 50:40; Matthew 10:14-15; 11:23-24; Luke 17:29; Revelation 11:8). It is apparent that homosexual behavior was not their only sin, but one of many. Ezekiel says that the people of Sodom "'*were arrogant, overfed and unconcerned; they did not help the poor and needy.*'" He further reports that they did *detestable things* before God (Ezekiel 16:49-50; 18:12; 33:26). The word *detestable* (*to'ebah*) also appears in the prohibitions against homosexual behavior in Leviticus 18:22 and 20:13. In addition, Jude says that *Sodom and Gomorrah and the surrounding towns gave themselves up to sexual immorality and perversion. They serve as an example of those who suffer the punishment of eternal fire* (Jude 7). The sexual license of Sodom and Gomorrah is also recounted by the apostle Peter (2 Peter 2:6-9).

---

[12]Compounded with the issue of avoiding sexual perversion (men with men), there is also the element of women being devalued as property in the ancient world. This was not God's original plan in the Creation, but resulted after sin came into the world.

In modern times, militant homosexuals often accuse those who oppose their practices of being judgmental, homophobic bigots. In some places, those who speak out against homosexuality have lost their jobs and have even been arrested. In the same way, the Sodomites railed against Lot for *playing the judge*. They were angry that some brave soul in their midst had the nerve to criticize their perverse behavior. Nevertheless, in the end, the Sodomites were destroyed and Lot was spared. He was rewarded for fearing God and calling sin "sin."

4. Contemptible Copulation (Leviticus 18, 20)

After God delivered Israel from Egyptian bondage in the Exodus, he gave them the Law through Moses at Mt. Sinai. Within that legal system, we find prohibitions against adultery, incest, bestiality, and also homosexuality. Leviticus 18:22 says, "'*Do not lie with a man as one lies with a woman; that is detestable.*'" Leviticus 20:13 further states, "'*If a man lies with a man as one lies with a woman, both of them have done what is detestable. They must be put to death; their blood will be on their own heads.*'"

These laws were written from an adult male perspective so they do not specifically deal with lesbianism. However, the spirit of the law would forbid that practice as well since it is also against God's created order.[13] Most likely, lesbianism was extremely rare in the second millennium B.C. and needed no specific prohibition. After all, the practice is not mentioned in texts from the Ancient Near East from that time period. Later, during the first millennium B.C., lesbianism became popular among the Greeks. Following this development, it was condemned by Jews and Christians alike (Romans 1:26).[14]

At this point, we will look at the specific wording of the more comprehensive prohibition in Leviticus 20:13. *If a man* (*'ish*) refers to an adult, not a minor. As previously noted, these laws were written from a man's perspective. Moreover, it was more likely for an adult to initiate sexual relations than it was a minor. *Lies with a man* (*zakar*) refers to a male of any age, whether a minor or an adult;[15] this prohibition is not limited to pederasty. *As one*

---

[13]Some may argue that lesbianism was acceptable since it did not have to involve penetration. However, using that same reasoning, one could justify a male fondling everyone he is forbidden to have intercourse with in Leviticus 18.

[14]*Pseudo-Phocylides* 190-192; Talmud *Shabbath* 65a; *Yebamoth* 76a.

[15]Talmud *Sanhedrin* 54a.

lies with a woman (*'ishshah*) is descriptive of sexual intercourse. It was natural for a man to lie with a woman; however, it was a perversion for him to lie with another male as he would with a woman.

Both of them emphasizes that each male is guilty, both the active and passive partner. *Have done what is detestable* (*to'ebah*) demonstrates the extreme offense that homosexual behavior is in the eyes of God. While the term *detestable* is generally applied to many of the sins in this section (Leviticus 18:26-30), it is only specifically applied to homosexuality (Leviticus 18:22; 20:13). *They must be put to death* points to the gravity of this sin; the death penalty was probably carried out by stoning.[16] *Their blood will be on their own head* stresses the fact that the offenders were personally responsible for their own destruction.

Some advocates of homosexuality try to minimize the force of the levitical commands by arguing that these were given in response to Canaanite practices or for the sake of ritual purity. They point out that this section of Scripture also says not to have sexual intercourse with a woman during her menstruation (Leviticus 18:19), not to wear a garment made from two types of material (Leviticus 19:19), and not to trim the corners of your beard (Leviticus 19:27). However, there is a monumental difference between those injunctions and the command prohibiting homosexuality. The former laws relate only to Israel, while the latter one belongs to the realm of moral law for all people. Homosexuality, along with bestiality (Leviticus 18:23), is against

[16]Stoning was the mode of capital punishment used for those who offered child sacrifices (Leviticus 20:2), mediums and spiritists (Leviticus 20:27), blasphemers (Leviticus 24:10-23), Sabbath violators (Numbers 15:32-36), and rebellious sons (Deuteronomy 21:18-21). According to Jewish tradition, stoning was also used for those who committed homosexual acts (Talmud *Niddah* 13b; *Sanhedrin* 54a; Mishnah *Sanhedrin* 7.4).

God's created order. The Jewish historian Josephus wrote, "But, then, what are our laws about marriage? That law owns no other mixture of sexes but that which nature has appointed, of a man with his wife. . . . But it abhors the mixture of a male with a male; and if any one does that, death is his punishment."[17]

Others argue that what is being forbidden is sacred prostitution. However, there is nothing in the prohibition that limits the detestable behavior to homosexual practice in a pagan worship setting. The only law in this context dealing with pagan worship forbids child sacrifice (Leviticus 18:21; 20:1-5). For one to consistently make such an argument, he would have to say that such sins as incest, adultery, and bestiality were also acceptable behaviors—as long as they were committed outside of a pagan worship setting.

Still others try to disregard the prohibitions against homosexuality because they are from the Old Covenant. While it is true that Christians live under the New Covenant, this does not mean that all of the laws given in the Old are irrelevant. Many laws found in the Old Testament contain permanent principles which were established at Creation, such as those condemning murder, theft, lying, adultery, and homosexuality (1 Timothy 1:8-11). These principles are repeated in the New Testament, demonstrating that the continuity of moral truth extends from the very beginning until the end of time.

The injunctions which appear in Leviticus 18 and 20 were given to Israel in order to protect God's original intention for marriage (Genesis 1-2). Many forms of illicit sexual activity, including adultery, homosexuality, and bestiality, are forbidden in Leviticus. These laws are presented in order to guard God's

---

[17]Josephus *Against Apion* 2.199.

sacred plan for sexual relations to be experienced by a man and a woman within the context of marriage.

5. Cross-dressing Countered (Deuteronomy 22)

In addition to forbidding homosexuality, the Law given to Israel also prohibited cross-dressing: "*A woman must not wear men's clothing, nor a man wear women's clothing, for the* LORD *your God detests anyone who does this*" (Deuteronomy 22:5). God intends for men and women to dress appropriately according to their gender. In Mesopotamia, male devotees of Ishtar who performed music, dances, and plays dressed as women and wore makeup. The goddess herself was believed to possess both male and female characteristics, being worshiped as "a charming, erotic woman" and as "a bearded soldier."[18]

Several descriptions of transvestism come down to us from the Greco-Roman period.[19] Effeminate men braided their long hair, plucked or shaved their body hair to make their skin soft, dressed in women's clothing, painted their faces with cosmetics, and drenched themselves with perfume.

The act of cross-dressing was closely associated with same-sex behavior. Sometimes homosexual men who played the passive role dressed as women, and lesbian women who played the active role appeared as men.[20] Further, devotees of certain pagan religions were known to cross-dress. For example, dedicated male followers of the goddess Cybele castrated themselves, donned women's clothing, and assumed feminine identities. These men who acted as women were known as Galli.[21]

Another illustration appears in this description from the

---

[18]Martii Nissinen, *Homoeroticism in the Biblical World: A Historical Perspective* (Minneapolis: Fortress Press, 1998), 30.

[19]Epictetus *Discourses* 3.24-35; Athenaeus *Deipnosophistae* 13.565; Josephus *Wars* 4.561-562; Philo *Special Laws* 3.37-42.

[20]Lucian *Dialogues of the Courtesans* 290-291.

[21]Lucian *The Syrian Goddess* 15, 26, 51.

Jewish philosopher Philo: "Certainly you may see these hybrids of man and woman continually strutting about through the thick of the market, heading the processions at the feasts, appointed to serve as unholy ministers of holy things, leading the mysteries and initiations and celebrating the rites of Demeter."[22] The fact that such wicked men make a pretense of holiness is a paradox indeed! Philo's description has not eluded us in modern times as "drag queens" flaunt their sinful pride, marching in parades which advocate homosexual perversion.

---

[22]Philo *Special Laws* 3.40.

6. Detestable Dogs (Deuteronomy 23)

The Law forbids those who would, whether heterosexually or homosexually, engage in so-called "sacred prostitution": *No Israelite man or woman is to become a shrine prostitute. You must not bring the earnings of a female prostitute or of a male prostitute into the house of the LORD your God to pay any vow, because the LORD your God detests them both* (Deuteronomy 23:17-18). Sacred prostitution was the most acceptable form of homosexuality in the Ancient Near East. Nevertheless, the LORD rejected this detestable practice too.

The first law (Deuteronomy 23:17) forbids an Israelite man or woman from becoming a *shrine prostitute* (*qadesh/qedeshah*), or "holy one." Sacred prostitution was practiced by the Canaanites and the surrounding nations (Genesis 38:21-22; Numbers 25:1-3). However, to the LORD, such relations were anything but holy. Shrine prostitutes engaged in sexual relations outside the sacred covenant of marriage, and sometimes they did this for money (see Micah 1:7).[23]

God warned his people not to participate in the sinful rites of the Canaanites whose land they would overtake (Leviticus 18:24-30). Nevertheless, the Israelites were frequently tempted to worship the LORD in pagan ways or turn away from him to worship the Canaanite fertility deities Baal and Ashtoreth/Asherah (Judges 2:13; 3:7). Female shrine prostitutes offered themselves to men at the high places, perhaps in order to magically stimulate fertility in the land (Jeremiah 2:20; 3:6;

---

[23] A Babylonian custom required every woman in the land to come to Aphrodite's (Ishtar's) temple once and have intercourse with a stranger. A man would cast money into the woman's lap in exchange for sex (Herodotus 1.199; see Strabo *Geography* 16.1.20).

Hosea 4:14). Male prostitutes were apparently used homosexually, as in the rest of the ancient world.[24] Often such men were intentionally castrated, and it was believed that the deity had changed their gender into that of a female. This pagan practice most likely serves as part of the rationale for the prohibition found in Deuteronomy 23:1: "*No one who is emasculated or has his male organ cut off shall enter the assembly of the* LORD" (NASB). God did not want these individuals corrupting the worship of his covenant people.

The second law (Deuteronomy 23:18) prohibits bringing the wages of a prostitute into the house of the LORD in order to pay a vow. This "dirty money" was unacceptable to God since it was acquired by sinful means. Perhaps the sacred prostitutes in the previous verse are the ones under consideration here. If this is the case, the various terms for male and female prostitutes would be used synonymously. Another possibility is that this second law is more general in its application. The term *female prostitute* (*zonah*) in verse 18 often refers to a common prostitute, whereas the word *qedeshah* in verse 17 refers to a *shrine prostitute.* Moreover, the term *male prostitute* (*keleb*) is used in verse 18, instead of *shrine prostitute* (*qadesh*) in verse 17.

The word *keleb* literally means "dog." It was often used as a term of derision denoting an individual's inferior status or shameless behavior. Here it refers to a man who engaged in homosexual prostitution. Some argue that the designation should be understood in a positive sense; a "dog" was a devoted, faithful servant of a god or goddess. However, it is better understood in light of the fact that it was humiliating for a male to be

---

[24]See Robert Gagnon, *The Bible and Homosexual Practice* (Nashville: Abingdon Press, 2001), 100-110; Will Roscoe, "Priests of the Goddess: Gender Transgression in Ancient Religion," *History of Religions* 35 (1996): 195-230.

penetrated—to play the part of a woman. Furthermore, the passive position of the homosexual act resembled that of a dog.[25]

The LORD considered the immoral behavior and unclean earnings of both male and female prostitutes as *detestable* (*to'ebah*). This term was previously used in the prohibitions against homosexuality in Leviticus 18:22 and 20:13. God is angered at paganism, prostitution, and homosexual behavior. These grievous sins stir up his jealous anger and righteous indignation (1 Kings 14:22-24).

---

[25]John B. Burns, "Devotee or Deviate: The Dog (*keleb*) in Ancient Israel as a Symbol of Male Passivity and Perversion," *Journal of Religion and Society* 2 (2000). Devotees of the goddess Ishtar, known as *assinnu*, *kurgarru*, and *kulu'u*, were represented by the cuneiform signs "man-woman," "dog-woman," and "phallus-buttocks." See Nissinen, 28, 32-33, 147 (n. 45), 150 (n. 88).

7. Vile Villains (Judges 19)

After Israel conquered the land of Canaan, they were governed by judges whom God periodically raised up to deliver his people from their enemies. This period is well known for its gross immorality. The conclusion of the book of Judges (17:1-21:25) emphasizes this very point and is bracketed with the phrase *everyone did as he saw fit* (Judges 17:6; 21:25).

Within this conclusion, we read the story about a Levite whose concubine had left him and returned to her father's house. The Levite made the journey to Bethlehem to convince her to return home with him. After several days of feasting with his father-in-law, the Levite finally set out for home in the hill country of Ephraim, being accompanied by his concubine and manservant. As nightfall came, the Levite chose to bypass Jerusalem because it was not inhabited by Israelites at that time; he did not feel secure in that place. The threesome finally arrived at Gibeah, an Israelite stronghold in which the travelers expected to find hospitality and safety. An old man found them in the city square and offered them a place to spend the night.

At this point, the story takes a tragic spiral downward into the depths of depravity. Judges 19:22-26 says,

> *While they were enjoying themselves, some of the wicked men of the city surrounded the house. Pounding on the door, they shouted to the old man who owned the house, "Bring out the man who came to your house so we can have sex with [know] him."*
>
> *The owner of the house went outside and said to them, "No, my friends, don't be so vile. Since this man is my guest, don't do this disgraceful thing. Look, here is my virgin daughter, and his concubine. I will bring them out to you now, and you can use them and do to them whatever you wish. But to this man, don't do such a disgraceful thing."*

But the men would not listen to him. So the man took his concubine and sent her outside to them, and they raped her and abused her throughout the night, and at dawn they let her go. At daybreak the woman went back to the house where her master was staying, fell down at the door and lay there until daylight.

In the end, the Levite's concubine died and this tragic event led to a civil war in Israel.

This story has many similarities to the Sodom and Gomorrah narrative. There are many repeated themes, such as inhospitality, homosexuality, and violence. The men of Gibeah wanted to shame the Levite by penetrating him like a woman. This action is described as *vile* and *disgraceful*. The term *disgraceful* (*nebalah*), also translated "folly," denotes wicked deeds that only a fool would perform. The vile men of Gibeah still shamed the Levite by raping his concubine, but this was viewed as a lesser offense since it was not homosexual.

8. Righteous Ruth (Ruth 1)

The story of Ruth shines forth as a gleam of light in the otherwise dark period of the Judges. A famine struck the land of Israel, leading a family from Bethlehem to migrate to the foreign land of Moab. The family consisted of Elimelech and Naomi, along with their two sons Mahlon and Kilion. While the family sojourned in Moab, the husband and father Elimelech died. His two sons married Moabite women, but then they also died. The widow Naomi was left alone without male support; only her two Moabite daughters-in-law remained with her. After hearing that Bethlehem had been blessed with food, Naomi decided to return home. Her daughters-in-law Orpah and Ruth traveled with her for some distance, but Naomi tried to persuade them to return home. Orpah took Naomi's advice, but Ruth adamantly refused.

But Ruth replied, "Don't urge me to leave you or to turn back from you. Where you go I will go, and where you stay I will stay. Your people will be my people and your God my God. Where you die I will die, and there I will be buried. May the LORD *deal with me, be it ever so severely, if anything but death separates you and me"* (Ruth 1:16-17).

This famous text is frequently read at modern wedding ceremonies and is applied to the commitment between a bride and groom. However, in its original context, the passage expresses the loyalty of a daughter-in-law toward her mother-in-law. Ruth was concerned that Naomi, an aged widow, could not survive alone. The Moabitess left her family, customs, religion, and native land in order to support her mother-in-law (Ruth 2:2, 11-12). In the process, she became a worshiper of the LORD and a model of his loving-kindness (*chesed*, Ruth 3:10).

Some lesbians, desperate for biblical approval, make the outrageous and slanderous claim that Ruth and Naomi were involved in a committed, sexual relationship. However, all of the evidence from the book of Ruth indicates that the two women were only involved in heterosexual relationships. Naomi had been married to Elimelech for many years and had given birth to two sons (Ruth 1:2). Ruth herself had been married to Naomi's son Mahlon, but had not borne him any children (Ruth 1:4; 4:10).

Naomi did not remarry because of her age; most men would not have been interested in her because she was too old to bear children (Ruth 1:12). However, Naomi made every effort to have her daughters-in-law remarried. She desired that both of them return to their Moabite homes in order to find a husband (Ruth 1:8-9). When Naomi kissed Orpah and Ruth, she did so to say "goodbye"—an act that resulted in weeping (Ruth 1:9, 14). Kissing was a common way to greet someone of the same gender; it certainly does not indicate that the women were lesbians!

Orpah took her mother-in-law's advice and probably found herself a Moabite husband. On the other hand, Ruth traveled back with Naomi to Bethlehem. It was Naomi who orchestrated the plan by which Ruth would find a secure home as the wife of Boaz (Ruth 3:1-4). After Boaz and Ruth were wed, the couple consummated the marriage and became the parents of Obed (Ruth 4:13). Through their lineage, King David was born (Ruth 4:17, 22).

9. Devoted David (2 Samuel 1)

Just as some lesbians misrepresent Ruth, so also some homosexuals misrepresent David. They contend that David was involved in a sexual relationship with Jonathan, the son of King Saul. Three different texts have been cited in support of this ludicrous accusation. The first text is 1 Samuel 18:1-4, which tells about a covenant made between the two men:

After David had finished talking with Saul, Jonathan became one in spirit with David, and he loved him as himself. From that day Saul kept David with him and did not let him return to his father's house. And Jonathan made a covenant with David because he loved him as himself. Jonathan took off the robe he was wearing and gave it to David, along with his tunic, and even his sword, his bow and his belt.

This passage treads on the heels of the story about David conquering the Philistine giant Goliath (1 Samuel 17). No doubt Jonathan felt great admiration for David's bravery and saw his potential as a leader in Israel. The text tells about the close friendship that developed between Jonathan and David and the covenant they made. The phrase *Jonathan became one in spirit with David* can be more literally translated "the soul of Jonathan was knit with the soul of David." This same expression is used to describe the great love that the patriarch Jacob had for his son Benjamin (Genesis 44:30-31).

The phrase *he loved him as himself* has no inherent sexual connotations either. After all, this statement resembles the command of God found in the Law to "'*love your neighbor as yourself*'" (Leviticus 19:18). The term *love* (*'ahab*) is general, being used for several kinds of relationships: love for a child (Genesis

22:2), love for a mate (Genesis 24:67), love for food (Genesis 27:4), love for God (Exodus 20:6), as well as love for one's neighbor (Leviticus 19:18). It is even used for the love that the people of Israel and Judah had for David (1 Samuel 18:16).

The fact that *Jonathan made a covenant with David* has no romantic connotations whatsoever—as if this were some kind of homosexual union or marriage. Instead, Jonathan promised his friendship and protection to David at all personal costs—giving him not only his robe and tunic,[26] but also his sword, bow, and belt! These acts had significant political overtones. It seems that Jonathan (the king's son) recognized that David (a shepherd) would someday rule over Israel, just as God ordained (1 Samuel 15:28; 20:12-15; 23:17). Although Jonathan was greater in status, he humbly recognized that David would someday be his superior. Jonathan's protection of David from the envious King Saul became a great source of contention between the father and son (1 Samuel 20:30-34).

The second text used to support the homosexual argument is 1 Samuel 20:41-42, where Jonathan and David kissed each other. In the context, Jonathan warned David of the dangerous threat posed by his father, King Saul. The kiss was used as a farewell; they wept at the fact that David had to go into hiding in order to save his life. A kiss was used as a common way to greet others of the same gender in ancient times (men-men,

---

[26]Homosexual interpreters envision Jonathan stripping to the point of total nakedness in order to erotically please David. This highly imaginative interpretation should be rejected on three grounds. First and foremost, there is absolutely no hint of eroticism in the text. Second, even if Jonathan took off his robe and tunic, there is no proof that he was not wearing a loin cloth or some other undergarment. Third, some translations render the term *tunic* (*mad*) as "armor," presenting it as a comprehensive term that includes the sword, bow, and belt (NKJV, NASB, RSV, NRSV, NJB). If this rendering is accurate, we cannot assume that Jonathan removed any of the clothing under his armor.

women-women), and is still customary in the Middle East. There are several examples of people who greet each other this way in both the Old and New Testaments: Joseph and his brothers (Genesis 50:1), Naomi and her daughters-in-law (Ruth 1:9), Samuel and Saul (1 Samuel 10:1), Absalom and the Israelites (2 Samuel 15:5), David and Barsillai (2 Samuel 19:39), Judas and Jesus (Matthew 26:49), and all the early Christians (Romans 16:16; 1 Corinthians 16:20). If the fact that David and Jonathan kissed means that they were sexual partners, then this logic would make almost every person in the Ancient Near East either a homosexual or a lesbian!

The third text, 2 Samuel 1:23-26, is an excerpt from David's lament for King Saul and his son Jonathan after they both died:

"Saul and Jonathan—in life they were loved and gracious, and in death they were not parted. They were swifter than eagles, they were stronger than lions. O daughters of Israel, weep for Saul, who clothed you in scarlet and finery, who adorned your garments with ornaments of gold. How the mighty have fallen in battle! Jonathan lies slain on your heights. I grieve for you, Jonathan my brother; you were very dear to me. Your love for me was wonderful, more wonderful than that of women."

Those who try to turn David into a homosexual seize upon the last sentence: "*Your love for me was wonderful, more wonderful than that of women.*" However, the term *love* (*'ahabah*) is related to the word found in 1 Samuel 18:1-4; it does not inherently refer to sexual love. The correct interpretation of this text involves the sacrificial love that Jonathan exhibited toward David. Jonathan humbly gave up his right to the throne of Israel so that his friend might become king. Jonathan could have betrayed David into the hands of King Saul, but instead he protected him. Jonathan had nothing to gain from his friendship with David, but he had everything to lose!

Women also loved David, but their affection led to their own personal gain. Their attachment to the king gave them the status of a queen and all the finery that accompanies such a title. They were brought into his palace and enjoyed the finest foods, clothing, and jewelry. Further, they received a certain amount of notoriety among the people of Israel.

It is noteworthy that David describes Jonathan as *my brother*. David did not love Jonathan romantically as he would a wife, but rather considered him as a male sibling. Their relationship illustrates the proverb which states that *there is a friend who sticks closer than a brother* (Proverbs 18:24).

There is absolutely no indication that David and Jonathan ever had homosexual relations. On the other hand, there is plenty of evidence that both men engaged in heterosexual intercourse. Although Jonathan's wife is not named in the Bible, much attention is given to his son Mephibosheth (2 Samuel 9). David himself was a lady's man, possessing many wives and concubines through whom he fathered numerous children. Among his wives, there was Michal, Ahinoam, Abigail, Maacah, Haggith, Abital, Eglah, and Bathsheba (1 Samuel 18:27; 1 Chronicles 3:1-9). The story of David's adultery with Bathsheba is well known. He first saw this voluptuous woman taking a bath on her rooftop, and then summoned her to his palace for sexual intercourse (2 Samuel 11:2-5). After arranging her husband's death in battle, King David took Bathsheba for his own wife. Near the end of his life, David had poor circulation and his body could not get warm. A beautiful young virgin named Abishag was summoned to sleep next to him and keep him warm, even though the two did not engage in sexual relations (1 Kings 1:1-4).

10. Radical Reformation (2 Kings 22-23)

As previously mentioned, the Law prohibited homosexual behavior (Leviticus 18:22; 20:13), including the practice of sacred prostitution (Deuteronomy 23:17-18). Nevertheless, during the chaotic period of the Divided Kingdom, homosexual prostitution repeatedly took root in Israel. The people of God had been adversely influenced by the Canaanites and the pagan nations surrounding them. The fact that male shrine prostitutes existed among God's people is highlighted as the epitome of wickedness.

During the days of King Rehoboam, the jealous anger of the LORD was provoked because of the dreadful evil done in Judah (1 Kings 14:23-24):

They also set up for themselves high places, sacred stones and Asherah poles on every high hill and under every spreading tree. There were even male shrine prostitutes in the land; the people engaged in all the detestable practices of the nations the LORD had driven out before the Israelites.

The people of Judah were behaving like Canaanites, committing the same detestable practices that led to their expulsion from the land. Rehoboam must have been negatively influenced by his pagan mother to allow these perversions. This is evident because the section is bracketed by the following statement: *His mother's name was Naamah; she was an Ammonite* (1 Kings 14:21, 31). Due to the people's sin, God allowed their enemies to ransack Jerusalem and carry off its treasures.

Sacred prostitution persisted throughout the reigns of Rehoboam and his son Abijah. However, Abijah's son Asa possessed a different spirit: *Asa did what was right in the eyes of the LORD, as his father David had done. He expelled the male shrine prostitutes from the land and got rid of all the idols his fathers had made* (1 Kings

15:11-12). Godly leadership requires bold decisions and actions; no doubt Asa's policies were not popular with all the people. However, he feared God and desired that his nation walk in the ways of the LORD. Apparently homosexual prostitution was so extensive and pervasive that it could not be eradicated overnight. Later, King Jehoshaphat finished the job: *He rid the land of the rest of the male shrine prostitutes who remained there even after the reign of his father Asa* (1 Kings 22:46).

Over time, the male shrine prostitutes made a comeback in Judah. Perhaps they plied their trade during periods where there is no record of the practice. Nevertheless, there is concrete evidence for their existence during the reign of King Josiah a few centuries later. It has been suggested that the notoriously wicked King Manasseh brought them back. The Bible records that he reintroduced many offensive things, including Baal altars, Asherah poles, worship of the starry hosts, child sacrifice, sorcery, and divination (2 Kings 21:1-15). Manasseh's grandson Josiah inherited a nation that was overrun by gross immorality.

While King Josiah was having the temple in Jerusalem renovated, the Book of the Law was found. After hearing this book read, he tore his clothes in grief because he realized how far the people had strayed from the LORD. God revealed to him that the nation would be laid waste for their rebellion. However, since Josiah humbled himself before God, this calamity would not take place in his lifetime. In response, the king initiated a radical reformation in which he dismantled pagan worship. He removed the pagan priests, cult sites, and sacred objects. Anything that was offensive to the LORD was smashed, burned, or desecrated. *He also tore down the quarters of the male shrine prostitutes, which were in the temple of the LORD and where women did weaving for Asherah* (2 Kings 23:7).

It is beyond human comprehension how the people of God could merge such offensive practices with divine worship! Jerusalem was the special location where God placed his divine Name. It was the site where the LORD's temple rested with his divine presence filling the Most Holy Place. And his people polluted his temple with the worship of pagan deities and their detestable practices! They had ignored God's divine revelation—even to the point of losing the Book of the Law.

There are some striking parallels to Judah found in modern times. Some people attempt to worship God while clinging to their sinful lifestyles. A few even claim to be "homosexual Christians," which is a complete contradiction in terms. To be a Christian means that a person is "a follower" or "slave of Christ." How can one claim to serve Christ, and then practice what he detests? Like the ancient people of Judah, many today have lost contact with the divine Book. They are either ignorant of the Bible's teachings or else they distort what it plainly says. Unlike Josiah, they have not torn their robes in repentance.

11. Premature Parting (Job 36)

The story of Job, found in the Wisdom Literature of the Old Testament, tells about a righteous man from the East who lost everything overnight, including his sons, daughters, servants, flocks, and herds. After all these tragedies, Job's own health was afflicted. His friends visited in order to bring him comfort, but their words proved to be more of a burden than a solace. After struggling through the meaning of his suffering, Job's health and prosperity were finally restored by God.

In one of the many speeches found in the book of Job, we read this obscure statement: "*The godless in heart harbor resentment; even when he fetters them, they do not cry for help. They die in their youth, among male prostitutes of the shrines*" (Job 36:13-14). A comparison is made between godless men and male shrine prostitutes; they both die while they are still young. Unfortunately, their lifestyles lead to premature death. The life spans of the sacred prostitutes were most likely shortened because of the diseases that are common to those who engage in promiscuous homosexual behavior.

One of the sad realities of sexual immorality today is that many people are infected by disease. Homosexual men have especially been affected by HIV (Human Immunodeficiency Virus) and AIDS (Acquired Immunodeficiency Syndrome); many of these have suffered immensely and tragically died. While HIV/AIDS may not be a specific divine judgment against homosexuals, it follows the cause-and-effect form of judgment.[27]

[27]See the excellent discussion by Wood and Dietrich, 267-84. While HIV/AIDS are prevalent among homosexual men, the diseases have also affected promiscuous heterosexuals, IV drug users, recipients of blood transfusions, faithful spouses of adulterers, and innocent children. Further, the diseases have not impacted lesbians to the same extent as homosexual men.

The apostle Paul warns us, *Do not be deceived: God cannot be mocked. A man reaps what he sows. The one who sows to please his sinful nature [flesh], from that nature [flesh] will reap destruction; the one who sows to please the Spirit, from the Spirit will reap eternal life* (Galatians 6:7-8). The prophet Hosea writes, "*They sow the wind and reap the whirlwind*" (Hosea 8:7). Further, the wise man asks this pointed question: *Can a man scoop fire into his lap without his clothes being burned?* (Proverbs 6:27). One's personal sin can have great physical, social, and spiritual consequences—even affecting others who are innocent!

For many people today, the answer to the HIV/AIDS crisis is a medicinal cure for the disease. However, while such a cure is desirable, it would treat the symptoms without addressing the causes; it would only be a band-aid solution. As long as people continue to engage in sexual immorality—both heterosexual and homosexual—the disease will continue to spread. The behaviors which lead to the proliferation of sexually transmitted diseases must be changed. The language of Ezekiel is highly appropriate for this situation: "*Say to them, 'As surely as I live, declares the Sovereign LORD, I take no pleasure in the death of the wicked, but rather that they turn from their ways and live*'" (Ezekiel 33:11).

12. An Honorable Husband (Hosea 2)

In the Old Testament, the LORD is portrayed as the husband of his wife Israel (Isaiah 54:5-7; 61:10; 62:5; Jeremiah 2:2; 31:32; Ezekiel 16:1-63). This metaphor is used even though God is spiritual, not physical. He is pictured as an honorable husband whose wife has been unfaithful. Israel had gone after other lovers, the Baals, stirring up the jealousy and righteous anger of the LORD. In the future, however, Israel would be restored by God's grace. The LORD promised, "*I will plant her for myself in the land; I will show my love to the one I called 'Not my loved one.' I will say to those called 'Not my people,' 'You are my people'; and they will say, 'You are my God'*" (Hosea 2:23).

It is significant that the LORD is never portrayed—even metaphorically—in a same-sex relationship with Israel as a male lover; such a portrayal would contradict his creative design. It was commonly believed that the pagan gods and goddesses engaged in immoral intercourse, whether heterosexual or homosexual. Such myths were invented to justify perverse human behavior. The people would argue, "If the gods do it, so can we." In contrast, the husband-wife relationship is the one that was created and affirmed by the LORD. This is the only model in which sexual relations are acceptable to him.

13. The Jewish Jesus (Matthew 19)

Today some proponents of same-sex behavior make the argument that Jesus did not condemn homosexuality. This assertion is inaccurate and misleading. While the words of Jesus do not specifically mention the practice, his life and teaching certainly denounce it indirectly. The most likely reason that Jesus did not directly confront homosexual sin is that most of his teaching was presented to Jewish audiences. By the first century, same-sex behavior was not common among the Jews, but was frequently practiced by the Gentiles (Romans 1).[28]

It is false reasoning to assume that Jesus' silence on this specific issue means acceptance. Jesus was silent on many other issues that he certainly would have opposed, including: gambling, child abuse, spouse abuse, kidnapping, torture, incest, rape, bestiality, and necrophilia. Even though the Gospels do not quote Jesus as saying "You shall not commit homosexual acts," there are several arguments that demonstrate his disapproval of same-sex behavior:

1) Jesus was a Jew who supported the Law. Jesus was born into this world as a Jew under the Law (Galatians 4:4). While Jesus often disputed with the religious leaders of his day over their man-made traditions, he correctly interpreted and upheld the law of God. In Matthew 5:17-18, Jesus said,

"Do not think that I have come to abolish the Law or the Prophets; I have not come to abolish them but to fulfill them. I tell you the truth, until heaven and earth disappear, not the smallest letter, not the least stroke of a

---

[28] *Sibylline Oracles* 3.584-600; *Letter of Aristeas* 152; Josephus *Antiquities* 15.23-30; Talmud *Kiddushin* 82a. Perhaps the Jewish people had learned their lesson by enduring the Babylonian Captivity, which was a judgment for their sins committed in Canaan—including homosexual perversion.

pen, will by any means disappear from the Law until everything is accomplished."

Jesus was certainly not ignorant of the complementary design of the first man and woman (Genesis 1-2). As the second person of the Trinity, he was an active agent in the creation of the world (John 1:1-3; 1 Corinthians 8:6; Colossians 1:15-17; Hebrews 1:1-3). Furthermore, Jesus was not unaware of the prohibitions against a man lying with another male (Leviticus 18:22; 20:13; Deuteronomy 23:17-18). He was present in the wilderness when these laws were given to Israel through God's servant Moses (1 Corinthians 10:4). There is no doubt that Jesus supported the foundational truths about marriage and sexual behavior found in the Law.

2) Jesus used Sodom and Gomorrah as an illustration of God's judgment. While these wicked cities were guilty of many other sins, God's destruction came on the heels of their homosexual perversion. He rained down burning sulfur on these places, completely destroying them. Jesus recognized that Sodom and Gomorrah were justly judged for their iniquity. He used them as the premier Old Testament example of God's judgment on the wicked (Matthew 10:14-15; 11:23-24; Luke 10:10-12; 17:28-29).

3) Jesus denounced all forms of illicit sexual behavior. Even though he did not specifically mention homosexuality, the practice is included under the umbrella of more general terms. Jesus taught,

"What comes out of a man is what makes him 'unclean.' For from within, out of men's hearts, come evil thoughts, sexual immorality, theft, murder, adultery, greed, malice, deceit, lewdness, envy, slander, arrogance and folly. All these evils come from inside and make a man 'unclean'" (Mark 7:20-23).

The term *sexual immorality* (*porneia*) refers to any sexual activity outside of a legitimate marriage between a husband and wife. Homosexuality would certainly be included within this range of meaning.[29] Moreover, the term *lewdness* (*aselgeia*) describes the behavior of those who lack sexual sensibility and restraint. The word is used once in the New Testament to describe the reckless homosexual behavior of the men who lived in Sodom and Gomorrah (2 Peter 2:7). In pagan literature it is used in connection with both effeminate homosexuals and sensual lesbians.[30]

4) Jesus reaffirmed the divine design for marriage. By reaffirming the divine design in creation, Jesus indirectly opposed the practice of homosexuality. Some Pharisees came and asked Jesus if a man could divorce his wife for any reason. Jesus responded,

> *"Haven't you read . . . that at the beginning the Creator 'made them male and female,' and said, 'For this reason a man will leave his father and mother and be united to his wife, and the two will become one flesh'? So they are no longer two, but one. Therefore what God has joined together, let man not separate"* (Matthew 19:4-6).

Jesus emphasized the permanence of marriage based on the account of creation (Genesis 1:27; 2:24). The Creator *made them male and female*, not male and male or female and female. *For this reason* signifies causation; since God created male and female, then it is natural for a man to leave his parents and be united to his wife. The male and female were designed to come together as *one flesh*. When a man and woman are united in marriage, God joins them together. He has never joined a man with a man or a

---

[29]See Deuteronomy 23:17-18 in the Septuagint where *porn-* words refer to both heterosexual and homosexual prostitution.

[30]Polybius *History* 36.15.2-4; Pseudo-Lucian *Affairs of the Heart* 28.

woman with a woman—for such an act would contradict his creative design.[31] Even if unprincipled politicians pass laws allowing same-sex marriage and corrupt clergymen officiate at the altar, such unions are not recognized or blessed by God!

5) Jesus called all sinners to repent. Many people today paint an inaccurate portrait of Christ; they only use the colors of kindness, tolerance, and acceptance to cover their canvas. There is no doubt that Jesus was kind to people and freely associated with the masses. Furthermore, he interacted with those who were rejected by mainstream society—the tax collectors and "sinners." However, such associations were not for the purpose of condoning their lifestyles, but to call them back to God (Matthew 21:28-32; Luke 5:31-32). Jesus showed people the love of God, taught them his divine truth, and then called them to obedience. The grace of God demonstrated through Christ must lead to genuine repentance, resulting in a transformed life (Titus 2:11-14).

At the beginning of Jesus' ministry, he began to preach, "*Repent, for the kingdom of heaven is near*" (Matthew 4:17). His associations with sinners often led to their restoration. For example, Jesus chose to spend time in the home of Zacchaeus, a man with a poor reputation in his community. In response, this tax collector offered to give half of his wealth to the poor and pay back four times the amount to anyone whom he had cheated (Luke 19:8). In addition, Jesus showed mercy to a woman caught in the very act of adultery. At the end of this story, he instructed her, "*Go now and leave your life of sin*" (John 8:11). This same message applies to all of those who engage in homosexual lust and intercourse today.

---

[31]The only viable alternative that Jesus presents to heterosexual marriage is celibacy (Matthew 19:10-12; see 1 Corinthians 7:7-9, 25-38).

Jesus gravely warned his generation, "*But unless you repent, you too will all perish*" (Luke 13:3, 5). He, more than any other biblical character, warned people about the reality of hell (Matthew 5:22, 29-30; 10:28; 13:42; 18:8-9; 23:33; 25:41, 46). Further, Christ denounced those cities in which he had performed many miracles because they refused to repent (Matthew 11:20). He also wept over the city of Jerusalem because its inhabitants did not possess believing and repentant hearts (Matthew 23:37-39; Luke 19:41-44). Repentance is a core element of the gospel message that is to be preached to the nations until the second coming of Christ (Luke 24:46-47). Without it, one cannot enter into the kingdom of God.

14. Unnatural Unions (Romans 1)

To better understand the current text under consideration, it is important to notice the broader context. In Romans 1-3, the apostle Paul emphasizes the need that all people have for Christ as their Savior. In Romans 1, the Gentiles need Christ for they have transgressed natural law. In Romans 2, the Jews need Christ for they have transgressed the Law of Moses. In Romans 3, both Gentiles and Jews are all under the dominion of sin and share a common need for salvation through Jesus Christ.

Having seen the broader picture, we will now focus our attention on Romans 1. In this text, Paul tells how the Gentiles gave up the true knowledge of God, neither giving him thanks nor glory. Instead, they began to worship idols that they had made with their own hands which resembled men, birds, animals, and reptiles (Romans 1:18-23). In reality, they had become their own gods, throwing off the sovereign rule of Almighty God.

As a byproduct of their rebellion against God, the Gentiles also rejected his design for their sexual relationships which originated at Creation. Paul writes,

> *Therefore God gave them over in the sinful desires of their hearts to sexual impurity for the degrading of their bodies with one another. They exchanged the truth of God for a lie, and worshiped and served created things rather than the Creator—who is forever praised. Amen.*
>
> *Because of this, God gave them over to shameful lusts. Even their women exchanged natural relations for unnatural ones. In the same way the men also abandoned natural relations with women and were inflamed with lust for one another. Men committed indecent acts with other men, and received in themselves the due penalty for their perversion* (Romans 1:24-27).

Because the Gentiles rejected God's sovereign authority, he *gave them over* to sexual immorality and the *degrading of their bodies.* They devalued their bodies, using them for purposes contrary to God's intentions. He created male and female to be brought together in the holy covenant of marriage. He designed sexual relations for their permanence, pleasure, and procreation. The Gentiles' "gender bending" coupled male with male and female with female—a spiritual, social, and biological corruption that does not fulfill God's purposeful design.

Such *shameful lusts* encompass both homosexual and lesbian behavior. Paul emphasizes the far reaching nature of this Gentile depravity: *Even their women exchanged natural relations for unnatural ones.* The term *women* (*theleiai*) can more literally be translated "females"; this word emphasizes gender regardless of age. Compared to males, females are usually known for their sexual sanity and restraint. Shockingly, even some females traded natural relations with males for perverse sexual acts with other females.

This practice, known as "lesbianism," takes its name from the Greek island of Lesbos where same-sex relations among females were prevalent.[32] The poetess Sappho was from Lesbos and her works were well known for their lesbian infatuations. The most common form of lesbian relationships was adult women coupled with other women of similar age.[33] Women engaged in kissing, fondling, and mutual masturbation. In some cases, female couples employed an artificial phallus which one partner strapped on in order to penetrate the other as a male

---

[32]Lucian *Dialogues on the Courtesans* 289.

[33]Mark D. Smith, "Ancient Bisexuality and the Interpretation of Romans 1:21-27," *Journal of the American Academy of Religion* 64 (1996): 238-43. There is a shred of evidence that women kept girls after the men-boys model (Plutarch *Lycurgus* 18.4). However, if this practice existed, it certainly was not widespread.

would.[34] There is also evidence from a vase painting for women using a double *olisbos* whereby both partners could be stimulated at the same time.

Paul states that those who engaged in same-sex relations had *exchanged natural relations for unnatural ones.* The term *unnatural* (*para phusin*) is more literally translated "against nature" or "contrary to nature." This phrase was frequently used by both Jewish and Gentile writers who argued that homosexuality is a violation of the created order.[35] It is noteworthy that the words "creation," "created things," and "Creator" appear in the immediate context (Romans 1:20, 25). Since Paul is dealing with Gentiles who had not received the Law, he does not quote from Genesis, Leviticus, or Deuteronomy. Instead, he appeals to the created order which they witnessed in nature.

The apostle Paul also emphasizes male perversion: *Men committed indecent acts with other men.* The term *men* (*arsenes*) can more literally be translated "males"; as in the case of the "females," the emphasis is on gender regardless of age. Males, burning with lust, traded natural relations with females for sex acts with other males.

One prominent, but not exclusive, form of homosexuality in the ancient world was pederasty. The Greek term *paiderastia* originally meant "love for boys." Slave boys would sometimes grant sexual favors to their masters, perhaps in appreciation for

---

[34]Pseudo-Lucian *Affairs of the Heart* 28; Lucian *Dialogues of the Courtesans* 292; Seneca the Elder *Controversiae* 1.2.23.

[35]Josephus *Against Apion* 2.275; Plutarch *Moralia* 751C-E; Plato *Laws* 1.636C; *Phaedrus* 251; Athenaeus *Deipnosophistae* 13.605; Pseudo-Lucian *Affairs of the Heart* 19-22. For similar references which employ the term "nature" (*phusis*), see Josephus *Against Apion* 2.199; Philo *Special Laws* 1.325; 2.50; 3.38; *The Contemplative Life* 59; *On Abraham* 135; Dio Chrysostom *Discourse* 7.149; Plato *Laws* 8.836C; Plutarch *Moralia* 990D-F. For an excellent explanation of the use of *phusis* in the New Testament, see Gagnon, 369-78.

their support. Male students also gave themselves sexually to philosophers in gratitude for their instruction. In addition, men would frequently visit the gymnasium in order to meet young lovers. They took advantage of the fact that these youths exercised in the nude; men preferred boys who were handsome and athletic, but who were not yet able to grow facial hair.[36]

Boys ranging from 12 to 18 were usually the "beloved" (*eromenos*), that is, the receptive partner in oral and anal sex. At times they wore long hair and dressed effeminately, playing the role of a woman. Adult men usually acted as the "lover" (*erastes*), that is, the penetrating partner.[37] If a man eventually married a woman, he often broke off his relationship with the boy.[38]

Paul was not unaware of such sexual perversion since he had grown up in Tarsus, a university town, and had widely traveled on his missionary journeys. Moreover, the apostle wrote the Roman letter from the notoriously immoral city of Corinth. The Christians in Rome whom Paul addressed were not ignorant of these perverse practices either. After all, most of the emperors who reigned over the Roman Empire engaged in homosexual behavior. Perhaps Nero is the best known for his debauchery. Suetonius wrote concerning him, "He castrated the boy Sporus and actually tried to make a woman of him; and he married him with all the usual ceremonies, including a dowry and a bridal veil, took him to his house attended by a great throng, and treated him as his wife."[39]

Some homosexual advocates today argue that Paul is only

---

[36]Cicero *Disputations* 4.70; Plutarch *Moralia* 751-752; Seneca *Epistles* 95.24.

[37]Grown men who were penetrated—that is, who played the woman's role—were looked down upon with reproach (Plato *Laws* 8.836E; Plutarch *Moralia* 751D-E).

[38]Catullus *Poems* 61.122-150.

[39]Suetonius *Lives of the Caesars: Nero* 28.

denouncing pederasty. In other words, they maintain that same-sex relations among consenting adults is acceptable behavior. This argument has no basis in fact. While Paul's denunciation of homosexual behavior does include the common Greco-Roman practice of pederasty, it is certainly not limited to it. Homosexual relationships among male adults were also common; in some instances two men even got married.[40] The apostle does not even bring up the subject of age in Romans 1.[41] As previously mentioned, his use of the term "males" (*arsenes*) emphasizes gender regardless of age. If Paul wanted to specify pederasty, there were plenty of Greek terms available for him to do so.

We must also remember that Paul condemns both lesbian and homosexual behavior. *In the same way* (*homoios*) links the two activities together. Since there is very little evidence for adult women having sexual relations with young girls, the pederasty argument is inconsistent and must be rejected. Further, we must also keep in mind Paul's emphasis on nature and the created order. It is not surprising that his use of the terms "females" (*theleiai*) and "males" (*arsenes*) matches the wording of Genesis 1:27 in the Septuagint: *And God created man, according to the image of God he created him, male [arsen] and female [thelu] he created them.* Certainly, the issue at stake is God's complementary design of the male and female genders.

Other homosexual supporters think that this text is simply a prohibition against cult prostitution, as in the case of Deuteronomy 23:17. However, there is nothing in the context

---

[40]See Smith, "Ancient Bisexuality and the Interpretation of Romans 1:21-27," 234-37; Juvenal *Satire* 2.117-142; Martial *Epigrams* 1.24; 12.42; Cicero *Philippic* 2.18.44-45.

[41]The issue involves gender, not age. As far as heterosexual marriage goes, it was not uncommon in the ancient world for adult men to marry teenage girls. This practice was true for Greeks, Romans, and Jews.

that limits same-sex activities to sacred prostitution. While Romans 1 deals with the practice of idolatry which leads to many other sins, it does not indicate that these sins were limited to a temple or shrine. The point is that the sins of the Gentile world were a result of abandoning the true knowledge of God—and the same is true today.

In their rebellion, the Gentiles created gods in their own fallen image. They attributed to these deities many forms of wickedness that are common to men. It was even believed that the gods and goddesses of the Greco-Roman pantheons engaged in same-sex behavior. A well known example is the myth of Zeus and Ganymede.[42] One account of the story portrays Ganymede as a handsome Trojan prince with whom the god Zeus fell in love. Zeus, disguised in the form of an eagle, kidnapped the youth and carried him off to Mt. Olympus. There Ganymede became Zeus' beloved and served as a cupbearer for the gods. The Gentiles created such myths in order to justify their own sinful behavior. Josephus writes that "[the Greeks] actually attributed to the gods the practice of sodomy . . . , thus inventing an excuse for the monstrous and unnatural pleasures in which they themselves indulged."[43]

Some who promote homosexuality today want to limit Paul's denunciation to those who are heterosexuals practicing homosexuality; they distinguish such individuals from people who are "constitutionally homosexual"—or "born gay." Such a person would be acting against his/her "sexual orientation."[44] However, Paul never made such a distinction! Instead, the

---

[42]Plato *Laws* 1.636C-D.

[43]Josephus *Against Apion* 2.275; see 2.242-254; Plato *Laws* 1.636C-D.

[44]Using this same faulty reasoning, one could reach the conclusion that if a "constitutional homosexual" abandoned same-sex relations and got married to someone of the opposite gender, then he/she would be sinning!

apostle treats all homosexual activity as rebellion against God and a perversion of his divine order.

As a result of rebelling against God's created order, men *received in themselves the due penalty for their perversion.* This cause-and-effect judgment probably refers to the sexually transmitted diseases which result from homosexual behavior. Disease is more easily spread among homosexual men because the anus was not designed by God to be penetrated. The female's vagina has natural fluids that serve as a lubricant during intercourse. The vaginal walls are also strong and flexible, features which facilitate both intercourse and childbirth. On the other hand, the anus is not as strong or flexible, being designed for the elimination of human waste. During homosexual intercourse, tissues in the anus are much more subject to tearing and bleeding. Through this process, infectious body fluids easily pass from one partner to the next.

After adding to the list of Gentile sins in Romans 1, Paul concludes the chapter by writing, *Although they know God's righteous decree that those who do such things deserve death, they not only continue to do these very things but also approve of those who practice them* (Romans 1:32). There is grave danger for those who engage in homosexuality. The fact that those who engage in same-sex behavior *deserve death* could refer to the death penalty, eternal separation from God in hell, or both.

However, it is not only the ones who participate in this perversion that are guilty. Those who *approve of those who practice* homosexuality are also in rebellion against God. Today, there are many who approve of and promote same-sex behavior, same-sex marriage, and same-sex marriage benefits. These include friends, lobbying groups, major corporations, politicians, and others. Such endorsements make sin more acceptable in our modern society and encourage others to participate in it. The words of the prophet Isaiah are appropriate here: *Woe to those who call evil good and good evil, who put darkness for light and light for darkness, who put bitter for sweet and sweet for bitter* (Isaiah 5:20).

15. Sinners Sanctified (1 Corinthians 6)

On Paul's second missionary journey he came to Corinth, a city in southern Greece (Achaia) well known for its sexual immorality. This characterization had developed well before the first century because of the "sacred prostitution" associated with the temple of Aphrodite. Further, since it was a port city connected to the harbors at Lechaeum and Cenchrea, many sailors stopped there long enough to enjoy a one night stand. As a result of all this immorality, the verb "Corinthianize" (*korinthiazomai*) was coined to refer to those who engaged in illicit sex. Moreover, the term "Corinthian girl" (*Korinthia kore*) was used to refer to a prostitute.

In the city of Corinth, the apostle shared the good news that Jesus Christ had died on the cross for their sins and proved his identity as the Son of God by being raised back to life. Some of the Corinthians put their faith in Jesus, repented of their sinful lifestyles, and were baptized (immersed in water) to receive the forgiveness of their sins (Acts 18:8; 1 Corinthians 1:14-16; see Mark 16:15-16; Acts 2:38). These new converts, indwelled by the Holy Spirit, comprised the church of God in Corinth.

Paul later wrote to the Corinthian church and reminded them of the changes that took place at their conversion:

Do you not know that the wicked will not inherit the kingdom of God? Do not be deceived: Neither the sexually immoral nor idolaters nor adulterers nor male prostitutes nor homosexual offenders nor thieves nor the greedy nor drunkards nor slanderers nor swindlers will inherit the kingdom of God. And that is what some of you were. But you were washed, you were sanctified, you were justified in the name of the Lord Jesus Christ and by the Spirit of our God (1 Corinthians 6:9-11).

Within this text, the apostle mentions several kinds of people who will not enter into heaven.[45] These individuals are described by the sinful behaviors that persist in their lives. Among these, he mentions *male prostitutes* (*malakoi*) and *homosexual offenders* (*arsenokoitai*). The NIV has translated these terms too narrowly. *Malakos* means "soft" or "effeminate," and could refer to any male, regardless of age, who allows himself to be penetrated by another male. There is nothing inherent in the term which would limit it to either prostitution or pederasty. It simply refers to the passive partner in homosexual intercourse who plays the part of a woman.[46]

The companion term *arsenokoites* refers to the active partner, that is, the penetrator. It is a compound word, being formed by "male" (*arsenos*) and "lie with" (*koite*); it means "lie with a male." This term was most likely coined from the prohibitions in the Septuagint which forbid a man to "*lie with a male [arsenos] as one lies with [koiten] a woman*" (Leviticus 18:22; 20:13).[47] Paul's warning excludes from the kingdom of God anyone who continues to engage in homosexual intercourse—whether passively or actively.

And that is what some of you were points to the fact that some of the Corinthian Christians used to engage in same-sex activities. Homosexual behavior is a conscientious choice, just as is fornication, adultery, and the other sins listed in this text. However, by the grace of God revealed in Christ, these believers no longer committed such perverse sins. They died to these sins

---

[45]Paul gives similar instruction in Galatians 5:19-21, where he denounces the works of the flesh. Although homosexuality is not specifically mentioned, the practice would certainly fall under the categories of *sexual immorality* (*porneia*) and *debauchery* (*aselgeia*).

[46]Aristotle *Problems* 4.26; Dionysius *Roman Antiquities* 7.2.4; Theocritus 7.105; Plato *Phaedrus* 239C; Plutarch *Moralia* 751D; *Lives: Caius Gracchus* 4.4.

[47]David F. Wright, "Homosexuals or Prostitutes?: The Meaning of αρσενοκοιται (1 Cor. 6:9, 1 Tim. 1:10)," *Vigiliae Christianae* 38 (1984): 125-53.

when they were united with Christ in baptism: *But you were washed, you were sanctified, you were justified in the name of the Lord Jesus Christ and by the Spirit of our God.*

A Christian has been cleansed by the saving blood of Christ and has been indwelled by the Holy Spirit. He has been set apart for God's special purpose and, despite his past sins, is declared righteous in God's sight. He must continue to say "no" to the temptations offered by the evil one. God will not allow a believer to be tempted beyond what he can handle; in each situation he will provide a way of escape (1 Corinthians 10:13). Whenever the Christian does sin, he has an avenue of grace through repentance and confession in prayer (1 John 1:5-2:2). However, if the believer chooses to return to a sexually immoral lifestyle, he cannot have fellowship with God or the church (1 Corinthians 5-6).

Several today have forsaken the homosexual lifestyle in order to follow Christ. This pathway is not always easy, but the rewards are eternal. There are several steps for the penitent homosexual to take in order to ensure success:

1) give up a homosexual identity for a Christian identity;
2) make a strong commitment to the lordship of Jesus;
3) spend time in Bible study and prayer;
4) become a part of an accountability group;
5) avoid old friends and scenes which bring temptation;
6) discard all music, movies, magazines, and mementos that symbolize the homosexual lifestyle;
7) learn to forgive yourself and those who have hurt you;
8) busy yourself with activities that honor God;
9) get Christian counseling if necessary;
10) continually remember the love of Christ and the promise of his return.

16. Marriage Modeled (Ephesians 5)

Traditional marriage between a man and a woman is reinforced by the imagery of Christ and his church.[48] Although Jesus was celibate while on earth, he referred to himself as *the bridegroom* (Matthew 9:15; 25:1-13). This metaphor is used to explain his relationship with the church, his *bride* (John 3:29; 2 Corinthians 11:2; Revelation 19:6-9; 21:2, 9; 22:17).

Paul develops this imagery by drawing an impressive parallel between Christ/church and husbands/wives (Ephesians 5:22-33). First, Paul addresses the wives, calling them to imitate the submissive spirit which the church has toward Christ:

Wives, submit to your husbands as to the Lord. For the husband is the head of the wife as Christ is the head of the church, his body, of which he is the Savior. Now as the church submits to Christ, so also wives should submit to their husbands in everything (Ephesians 5:22-24).

Next, the apostle challenges husbands to imitate Christ in his sacrificial love for the church:

Husbands, love your wives, just as Christ loved the church and gave himself up for her to make her holy, cleansing her by the washing with water through the word, and to present her to himself as a radiant church, without stain or wrinkle or any other blemish, but holy and blameless. In this same way, husbands ought to love their wives as their own bodies. He who loves his wife loves himself. After all, no one ever hated his own body, but he feeds and cares for it, just as Christ does the church—for we are members of his body (Ephesians 5:25-30).

---

[48]This parallel resembles the one between the LORD and Israel in the Old Testament (Hosea 2).

Finally, Paul grounds this special relationship in Creation by quoting Genesis 2:24:

"For this reason a man will leave his father and mother and be united to his wife, and the two will become one flesh." This is a profound mystery—but I am talking about Christ and the church. However, each one of you also must love his wife as he loves himself, and the wife must respect her husband" (Ephesians 5:31-33).

It is significant that Christ is portrayed as a husband and the church as his wife. The writers of the New Testament would never portray the sinless Christ in a homosexual relationship.[49]

[49]The suggestion that Jesus and the beloved disciple (John 13:23; 19:26; 21:7, 20) were sexual partners is nothing short of blasphemy. Perhaps due to their upbringing, some homosexuals have a difficult time envisioning close relationships that do not involve sexual intercourse.

17. Rebels Restrained (1 Timothy 1)

Even though Christians are under a new covenant with Christ, there is still value in studying the teachings of the Old Testament. After all, there are some permanent precepts that span time, originating at the Creation and extending to the second coming of Christ. In Paul's letter to the evangelist Timothy, he writes these comments concerning the value of the Law:

We also know that law is made not for the righteous but for lawbreakers and rebels, the ungodly and sinful, the unholy and irreligious; for those who kill their fathers or mothers, for murderers, for adulterers and perverts, for slave traders and liars and perjurers—and for whatever else is contrary to the sound doctrine that conforms to the glorious gospel of the blessed God, which he entrusted to me (1 Timothy 1:9-11).

Within this list of rebellious sinners, we find those who are called *perverts* (*arsenokoitai*). This is the same Greek word that is rendered *homosexual offenders* in 1 Corinthians 6:9. As previously explained, *arsenokoites* is a compound term which denotes a man who lies with another male. Paul clearly points out that this immoral activity is condemned by the Law (Leviticus 18:22; 20:13). The Law was given by God as a deterrent to such perverse behavior.

The vice list in this text is introduced by three general couplets of those who demonstrate an affront to God: *lawbreakers and rebels, the ungodly and sinful,* and *the unholy and irreligious.* After these, the descriptions match numbers five through nine of the Ten Commandments (Exodus 20:12-16):

5) *"Honor your father and mother" / for those who kill their fathers or mothers,*

6) *"You shall not murder" / for murderers,*

7) *"You shall not commit adultery" / for adulterers and perverts,*

8) *"You shall not steal" / for slave traders,*[50]

9) *"You shall not give false testimony" / and liars and perjurers.*

The apostle closely associates homosexual perversion with adultery (see 1 Corinthians 6:9).[51] Both of these sins defy God's creative intent for sexual relations; intercourse is designed for a male and female to enjoy within the context of marriage.

[50]The term *slave traders* (*andrapodistai*) can also be translated "kidnappers." Sometimes these men abducted free citizens and sold them into slavery (Philo *Special Laws* 4.13-19). These facts explain the connection between *slave traders* and the eighth commandment against stealing.

[51]Under Philo's discussion of the seventh commandment against adultery, he also discusses homosexual behavior (*Special Laws* 3.37-42). The same is true in *Pseudo-Phocylides* 3: "Neither commit adultery nor rouse homosexual passion."

18. The Righteous Rescued (2 Peter 2)

The apostle Peter encouraged his Christian readers to continue in the true faith and to be on their guard against false teachers. He reassured them that God's justice would ultimately prevail and the wicked would be punished. Peter illustrated this principle by reminding them that God saved Lot, but destroyed Sodom and Gomorrah:

[For if God] condemned the cities of Sodom and Gomorrah by burning them to ashes, and made them an example of what is going to happen to the ungodly; and if he rescued Lot, a righteous man, who was distressed by the filthy lives of lawless men (for that righteous man, living among them day after day, was tormented in his righteous soul by the lawless deeds he saw and heard)—if this is so, then the Lord knows how to rescue godly men from trials and to hold the unrighteous for the day of judgment, while continuing their punishment. This is especially true of those who follow the corrupt desire of the sinful nature [flesh] and despise authority (2 Peter 2:6-10).

The ancient cities of Sodom and Gomorrah serve as an example of those who live immoral, unrepentant lives. A few key phrases describe their depravity: *filthy lives of lawless men, lawless deeds, corrupt desire of the sinful nature,* and *despise authority.* The word *filthy* (*aselgeia*) refers to their lack of sexual sensibility and restraint.[52] It appropriately describes the Sodomites who lusted after the visitors to their city, desiring to homosexually abuse them. Just as Sodom and Gomorrah were reduced to ashes, the wicked will also perish.

[52]This term previously appeared in the discussion on Jesus' teaching in Mark 7:20-23. In that text, *aselgeia* is translated *lewdness.*

Lot serves as an example to faithful believers who are frustrated by the wicked culture in which they live. Lot was distressed by the immorality and perversion of the Sodomites; he endured their sinful behavior day after day. When he expressed disapproval of their evil deeds, they mocked him for "playing the judge." Just as Lot was delivered from Sodom, faithful believers will also be saved from this world.

19. An Infinite Inferno (Jude)

Like the apostle Peter, Jude also used Sodom and Gomorrah as an example of gross evil and divine punishment: *In a similar way, Sodom and Gomorrah and the surrounding towns gave themselves up to sexual immorality and perversion. They serve as an example of those who suffer the punishment of eternal fire* (Jude 7). *Sexual immorality* (*ekporneuo*) may encompass all types of sexual intercourse performed outside of marriage. The companion term *perversion* is translated from a Greek phrase which is more literally rendered "went after other flesh." This is a reference to homosexual lust, an unnatural vice. The idea is that these wicked men were not satisfied with women, so they went after other men.

Some scholars think that "other flesh" has to do with the Sodomites' desire to have sexual relations with angels. However, the phrase "went after other flesh" relates not only to Sodom (where the two angels came), but also to Gomorrah and their neighboring towns. Further, the men of Sodom were ignorant of the fact that the two men were really angels (Genesis 19:4-5).

Sodom and Gomorrah were burnt to ashes for their fornication and homosexual perversion. They serve as an example to later generations who rebel against God. We should be warned that those who follow in their perverse footsteps will *suffer the punishment of eternal fire.*

20. Evildoers Expelled (Revelation 21-22)

Near the end of Revelation, the dwelling of God is with his faithful people. However, those who do evil are expelled from his presence. God declares, "*But the cowardly, the unbelieving, the vile,*[53] *the murderers, the sexually immoral, those who practice magic arts, the idolaters and all liars—their place will be in the fiery lake of burning sulfur. This is the second death*" (Revelation 21:8). Along with many others, the *sexually immoral* (*pornoi*) are consigned to eternal punishment. This broad category would include homosexuals and lesbians.

In the final chapter, Jesus also contrasts the ultimate fate of the saved with that of the lost:

> "*Blessed are those who wash their robes, that they may have the right to the tree of life and may go through the gates into the city. Outside are the dogs, those who practice magic arts, the sexually immoral, the murderers, the idolaters and everyone who loves and practices falsehood*" (Revelation 22:14-15).

Those who have been cleansed from sin by the blood of Christ are given eternal life inside the gates of heaven. In contrast, those who practice evil must remain outside the blessed city. These include *the dogs*, a term used for those who are spiritually unclean (Matthew 7:6; Philippians 3:2; 2 Peter 2:22). It is noteworthy that this same description was used in Deuteronomy 23:18 to designate male prostitutes who offered themselves to other men to be used homosexually. Revelation 22:15 also refers to the *sexually immoral* (*pornoi*) who are expelled from the presence of God.

---

[53] *The vile* translates a participle form of the Greek verb *bdelussomai*. The related noun *bdelugma* is used by the Septuagint in passages which label homosexual practice as *detestable* (Leviticus 18:22; 20:13; Deuteronomy 23:18).

Conclusion

There is nothing said in the whole Bible that is favorable toward homosexuality; every passage in both the Old and New Testaments that addresses the practice condemns it.[54] From the creation narrative (Genesis 1-2) to the scene of the final judgment (Revelation 21-22), homosexuality is prohibited. Under God's covenant with Israel, those who engaged in homosexual acts were to be stoned. Under his new covenant with Christians, those who persist in same-sex behavior are to be withdrawn from the fellowship of the church. Ultimately, those who are unrepentant will be eternally condemned.

There are two basic strategies that homosexuals use in an attempt to neutralize the biblical testimony. The first strategy is to grossly misinterpret the various passages that address same-sex behavior. Peter warned against such persons who twist the Scriptures *to their own destruction* (2 Peter 3:16). The other strategy is to deny the supreme authority of Scripture (2 Timothy 3:16-17), making the prohibitions against homosexuality irrelevant for our modern culture. However, *the faith . . . was once for all entrusted to the saints* (Jude 3) and it cannot be altered.

After surveying the various biblical texts that address homosexuality, the following conclusions can be made:

1) Sexual intercourse is reserved for a man and a woman within the bond of marriage. It was divinely designed for the permanence of their marriage, for their own pleasure, and for the procreation of children. It is a good gift from God to be enjoyed by a husband and his wife.

---

[54]This understanding of Scripture was universally accepted until modern times. Every ancient Jewish and Christian writer outside the Bible who mentions homosexual behavior condemns it (see *Appendix*).

2) Homosexual relations are not a part of the created order. Same-sex behavior is not a part of God's design and is not a gift from him. Like idolatry and other sins, homosexuality resulted from rebellion and pride.

3) Homosexual relations are incompatible with God's design. They do not conform to his plans for the spiritual, social, and biological unity of a man and a woman; homosexuality is "contrary to nature."

4) Homosexuality is not genetic; no one has ever been "born gay" or "born lesbian." Same-sex behavior is a choice, as is all sexual behavior. Even if a person is tempted with homosexual desires, he can resist these.

5) All homosexual lusts and behaviors are offensive to God. These activities are "detestable" to him. There are no exceptions to this rule.

6) The Bible makes no distinctions between wholesome and unwholesome same-sex relationships. All same-sex relationships are inherently evil, even if two people love each other and are lifelong partners.

7) Committed "love" does not justify same-sex behavior. The same rationalization could also be used to justify fornication and adultery. If a person truly loves another, that individual will not engage in any activity that will jeopardize the other person's eternal salvation.

8) Those who persist in homosexual behavior will be eternally condemned. Repentance is a key element in obedience to the gospel; without it one cannot receive the blessings of Christ's salvation. People repented of same-sex acts when they became Christians in the first century; several are doing the same today.

9) Those who condone homosexual behavior will be eternally condemned. It is wrong not only to participate in sin, but also to approve of it. People must repent of their endorsement of homosexuality.

10) God has the power to forgive all people through Jesus Christ. The power of Jesus' blood that was shed on the cross can cleanse the vilest of sinners. God does not want anyone to perish, but wants everyone to repent.

If modern people are not genetically homosexual, then why do some choose to engage in same-sex behavior? There are various reasons for this phenomenon, most of which relate to one's socialization. In the end, however, the individual makes his own choice. Some of the following factors may influence one's actions:

1) Rebellion against God. Defiance against God and his creative design are at the core of homosexual behavior. Those who engage in same-sex acts are not walking in the fear the LORD. They are rejecting the plain teaching of both nature and Scripture.

2) The influence of an ungodly culture. Modern youth are growing up in a world that idolizes sexual experimentation. Media sources such as television, music, movies, magazines, and the internet have frequently been a tool in the hand of Satan to promote fornication and adultery; now these same sources encourage homosexuality. The number of television shows and movies that portray same-sex couples is always increasing. In addition, the internet has made same-sex pornography much more accessible.

It is noteworthy that rates of homosexual behavior are higher in places where there is more social acceptance. Such negative influences are multiplying in urban areas which have liberal teachers that indoctrinate the naïve through "diversity" education. Beyond this, gay and lesbian clubs can be found at public high schools and state university campuses, beckoning rejected and lonely souls into their fold.

3) *Poor relationships with parents.* Children who do not feel affirmed by their parents may seek to find acceptance from same-sex relationships. This is especially true for boys who have problems with their fathers and girls who have difficulties with their mothers. The parents might be absent, emotionally unavailable, angry, overly demanding, perfectionists, or workaholics. Divorce or the death of a parent may also contribute to the problem. It could also be that the parents served as poor role models for their respective gender.

4) *A challenging boyhood.* If a boy does not enjoy the social processes involved in becoming a man, he may seek acceptance through homosexual relationships. Perhaps he has poor hand-eye coordination and is not athletically inclined. As a result, he is bullied by the more masculine boys and they call him a "sissy," "fag," or "queer." He begins to think of himself in these ways; these labels become a self-fulfilling prophecy. He makes friends among the girls and adopts their mannerisms and tastes. Further, he becomes attracted to the person he wishes he was—a strong, athletic man.

5) *Sexual abuse.* Such violence can have an adverse impact on how victims view themselves, others, and sexuality. A boy who is repeatedly sodomized may later in life view himself as a homosexual. On the other hand, a girl who is raped may come to distrust all men and find her security in a lesbian relationship. This latter phenomenon also occurs in the lives of adult women who have been abused emotionally, physically, or sexually by men. After being heterosexually active for many years—even in marriage—they may turn to lesbianism to find security and understanding.

6) Involvement with drugs and alcohol. Some people have no doubt been introduced to homosexual behavior through wild parties, which perhaps included group sex. The effects of drugs and alcohol, which distort one's judgment, served as a catalyst for their deviant behavior.

7) Poor religious role models. Some religious leaders today are openly living a homosexual lifestyle. By their own example and teaching they are leading many people astray, condoning what the Bible emphatically calls "sin." Other leaders, although not practicing homosexuals, also approve of this detestable behavior. All of these wolves in sheep's clothing make the rebellious feel at peace with God, instead of calling them to repentance.

8) A desire for love and acceptance. Perhaps some have been lured into a same-sex relationship because they were lonely or hurt and someone of the same gender offered them companionship and comfort. Teenage boys are sometimes approached by older men who monopolize on their insecurities. Although downplayed by activists, pederasty is still a common form of homosexuality today.

9) Natural sexual outlets are unavailable. Some people turn to homosexuality as an alternative when they cannot release their passion heterosexually. This phenomenon occurs among inmates confined in prison and sailors set out to sea. Such shameful behavior is also prevalent among Catholic priests who have taken a vow of celibacy. Several of these men have molested altar boys and other young children placed in their care.

10) An extreme form of feminism. Lesbianism takes the feminist ideology to its most radical height, rejecting traditional roles for women. Radical feminism rejects male dominance and leadership. In a lesbian relationship, there is no need to submit to the authority of a husband. Radical feminism also devalues the sacred role of motherhood. In a lesbian relationship, one cannot bear and rear children—except by artificial means.

Many who engage in same-sex behavior argue that it is "natural to them." However, as previously stated, no one is born a homosexual. One might choose this lifestyle over time, but this is not "natural" in the sense of God's creative design. Further, many people enslaved by various sins could make the same argument in order to justify their behavior, whether they be liars, thieves, arsonists, drunkards, or murderers. If people participate in sin long enough, it becomes "second nature" to them. An individual can have his conscience *seared as with a hot iron* so that he is no longer sensitive to God's truth (1 Timothy 4:2).

The homosexual lifestyle has worsened our quality of life around the globe. It, along with several other maladies, is a threat to the traditional (God-ordained) family which consists of Dad, Mom, and the kids. As homosexuality gains more and more acceptance, there will be an increase in the number of people who are swept into its clutches. Young people will become increasingly confused about their own gender roles and sexuality.

This aberrant lifestyle is well known for its weakness and instability. Homosexuals are notorious for their multiplicity of sex partners which can range in the hundreds or thousands over a lifetime. While promiscuity among lesbians is less extreme, several of these women also have sexual relations with men; they are bisexual. Homosexual men are known for having anonymous and group intercourse in bathhouses and sex clubs. Such unstable relationships lead many homosexuals into depression, substance abuse, domestic violence, and suicide.

Since homosexual men engage in unnatural behaviors[55] and are often promiscuous, they have contracted numerous diseases and received many physical injuries. The following diseases are common to those who practice sodomy: Human Immunodeficiency Virus (HIV), Herpes Simplex Virus (HSV), Human Papilloma Virus (HPV), anal cancer, Chlamydia Trachomatis, Gonorrhea, Syphilis, and Hepatitis A, B, and C. Other medical problems that result from sodomy include: Anogenital warts, hemorrhoids, anal fissures, and anorectal trauma. Oral-anal contact has also led to numerous gastrointestinal infections; the symptoms are now known as "the Gay Bowel." Lesbians are also susceptible to sexually transmitted diseases and other medical problems, even if they are not bisexual. These maladies include: Herpes Simplex Virus (HSV), Human Papilloma Virus (HPV), Trichomoniasis, and Anogenital warts.[56]

As a result of same-sex behavior, hundreds of thousands of men have suffered from HIV and died from AIDS. Even with this threat of death looming over them, most homosexual men still engage in anal sex. In order to fulfill their passionate lusts, they are willing to risk approximately 25 years of their life expectancy. In addition, it is not uncommon for those who have tested positive for HIV to continue their behavior without ever warning their sex partners. Despite "safe sex" campaigns, many infected men still engage in sodomy without a condom—a risky practice they refer to as "barebacking."

---

[55]Male homosexual behavior includes the following kinds of contact: oral-genital (oral sex), genital-anal (sodomy), oral-anal (rimming), hand-anal (fisting). Further, artificial sex toys are used such as anal plugs and vibrators. Other sadistic practices include the use of whips, ropes, and body harnesses.

[56]John Shea and John Wilson, "'Gay Marriage' and Homosexuality: Some Medical Comments" (www.catholiceducation.org/articles/homosexuality/ho0095.html); John R. Diggs, Jr., "The Health Risks of Gay Sex" (www.catholiceducation.org/articles/homosexuality/ho0075.html).

Homosexual behavior has been the key catalyst for the spread of HIV/AIDS in the United States. In response to this epidemic, the government is spending billions of dollars each year to care for those who have contracted these diseases. The taxpayers' dollars are being spent on prevention programs, HIV testing, medical treatment, pharmaceuticals, counseling, dental care, and housing. A large amount of money is given to metropolitan cities that have been disproportionately impacted by HIV/AIDS. The idea that homosexual sex is a private affair that does not affect anybody else is a myth of epic proportions.

In light of all these facts, there are many questions that both politicians and the general populace should ask themselves:

1) Why should we promote legal policies in favor of homosexuality when it is destroying us socially (unstable relationships), physically (disease), economically (health care funding), and spiritually (separation from God)?

2) Why should we promote marriage between two people of the same gender when it is an abomination to the Author of marriage?

3) Why should we allow same-sex couples to adopt children for whom they are unfit role models? Are we not concerned for the mental, physical, and spiritual safety of our children? These innocent souls might be led into the same perverted sexual patterns.

4) Why should we grant marriage-like benefits to partners of homosexuals? Not only do these people want to live in sin, they want others to pay for it.

5) What if everyone exclusively practiced homosexuality? The end result would be the destruction of the human race. There would be no more children born into the world. Many of those already alive would meet a premature death because of

sexually transmitted disease. The traditional family would be destroyed.

6) What if sexual relations were practiced only within the confines of heterosexual marriage according to God's plan? There would be no illegitimate children which would also result in a significant decrease in gang activity, drug abuse, and juvenile delinquency. Sexually transmitted diseases would eventually be eliminated. Occurrences of HIV/AIDS would be rare and less people would meet a premature death. Fewer burdens would be placed on the shoulders of health care providers and insurance companies. The federal government would save billions of dollars on social welfare and AIDS relief each year. Most importantly, God would be honored.

It is both Christian and patriotic to desire that righteousness prevails in one's own country. We should desire the physical health of others, encouraging the prevention of diseases that result from immoral behavior. We should desire the spiritual health of others, encouraging them to avoid activities that God detests. We should want our nation to thrive for many centuries into the future. The wise man once wrote, *Righteousness exalts a nation, but sin is a disgrace to any people* (Proverbs 14:34). The Canaanites were vomited out of their land for such wicked behavior (Leviticus 18:24-30). We do not want the same judgment to fall on us.

SELECTED BIBLIOGRAPHY

BOOKS

Davies, Bob and Lori Rentzel. *Coming Out of Homosexuality.* Downers Grove, Ill.: InterVarsity Press, 1993.

Gagnon, Robert. *The Bible and Homosexual Practice.* Nashville: Abingdon Press, 2001.

Smith, F. LaGard. *Sodom's Second Coming.* Eugene, Ore.: Harvest House Publishers, 1993.

Wold, Donald. *Out of Order: Homosexuality in the Bible and the Ancient Near East.* Grand Rapids, Mich.: Zondervan, 1998.

Wood, Glenn G. and John E. Dietrich. *The AIDS Epidemic: Balancing Compassion and Justice.* Portland, Ore.: Multnomah Press, 1990.

INTERNET ARTICLES

Cameron, Paul. "What Causes Homosexual Desire and Can It Be Changed?" (www.biblebelievers.com/Cameron3.html)

Diggs, John R. Jr. "The Health Risks of Gay Sex." (www.catholiceducation.org/articles/homosexuality/ho0075.html)

Shea, John and John Wilson. "'Gay Marriage' and Homosexuality: Some Medical Comments." (www.catholiceducation.org/articles/homosexuality/ho0095.html)

JOURNAL ARTICLES

Burns, John B. "Devotee or Deviate: The Dog (*keleb*) in Ancient Israel as a Symbol of Male Passivity and Perversion." *Journal of Religion and Society* 2 (2000).

DeYoung, James B. "The Contributions of the Septuagint to Biblical Sanctions Against Homosexuality." *Journal of the Evangelical Theological Society* 34 (1991): 157-77.

________. "A Critique of Prohomosexual Interpretations of the Old Testament Apocrypha and Pseudepigrapha." *Bibliotheca Sacra* 147 (1990): 437-54.

________. "The Meaning of 'Nature' in Romans 1 and Its Implications for Biblical Proscriptions of Homosexual Behavior." *Journal of the Evangelical Theological Society* 31 (1988): 429-41.

Malick, David E. "The Condemnation of Homosexuality in 1 Corinthians 6:9." *Bibliotheca Sacra* 150 (1993): 479-92.

________. "The Condemnation of Homosexuality in Romans 1:26-27." *Bibliotheca Sacra* 150 (1993): 327-40.

Roscoe, Will. "Priests of the Goddess: Gender Transgression in Ancient Religion." *History of Religions* 35 (1996): 195-230.

Smith, Mark D. "Ancient Bisexuality and the Interpretation of Romans 1:21-27." *Journal of the American Academy of Religion* 64 (1996): 223-56.

Thompson, J. A. "The Significance of the Verb *LOVE* in the David-Jonathan Narratives in 1 Samuel." *Vetus Testamentum* 24 (1974): 334-38.

Ukleja, P. Michael. "Homosexuality and the Old Testament." *Bibliotheca Sacra* 140 (1983): 259-66.

________. "Homosexuality in the New Testament." *Bibliotheca Sacra* 140 (1983): 350-58.

Wright, David F. "Homosexuality: The Relevance of the Bible." *Evangelical Quarterly* 61 (1989): 291-300.

________. "Homosexuals or Prostitutes?: The Meaning of αρσενοκοιται (1 Cor. 6:9, 1 Tim. 1:10)." *Vigiliae Christianae* 38 (1984): 125-53.

APPENDIX:
Ancient Judeo-Christian Literature

Every ancient Jewish and Christian writer outside the Bible who mentions homosexual behavior condemns it.

1. Apocrypha

Wisdom of Solomon 14.22-26

2. Pseudepigrapha

Jubilees 20.5

Testament of Levi 14.6

Testament of Levi 17.11

Testament of Naphtali 3.4

2 Enoch 10.4

2 Enoch 34.1-3

Letter of Aristeas 152

Sibylline Oracles 2.73

Sibylline Oracles 3.182-187

Sibylline Oracles 3.584-600

Sibylline Oracles 3.764

Sibylline Oracles 3.429-433

Pseudo-Phocylides 3

Pseudo-Phocylides 187

Pseudo-Phocylides 190-192

Pseudo-Phocylides 210-214

3. Philo

On Abraham 135-138

Special Laws 1.325

Special Laws 2.50

Special Laws 3.37-42

Contemplative Life 59-62

4. Josephus

Against Apion 2.199

Against Apion 2.275

Antiquities 1.200-201

Antiquities 4.290

Antiquities 15.29

Wars 4.561-563

5. Mishnah

Sanhedrin 7.4

6. Babylonian Talmud

Niddah 13b

Kiddushin 82a

Shabbath 65a

Yebamoth 76a

Sanhedrin 54ab

Sanhedrin 58a

Sanhedrin 70a

7. Midrash Rabbah

Genesis Rabbah 18.5

Genesis Rabbah 26.5

Genesis Rabbah 50.7

Leviticus Rabbah 23.9

8. Ante-Nicene Fathers

Didache 2.2

Epistle of Barnabas 10

Epistle of Barnabas 19

Epistle of Polycarp 5

Justin Martyr *Apology* 1.27

Aristides *Apology* 9

Aristides *Apology* 13

Theophilus *To Autolycus* 1.2

Apocalypse of Paul 39

Clement *Instructor* 3.3

Clement *Exhortation to the Heathen* 2

Methodius *Banquet of the Ten Virgins* 5.5

Tertullian *The Crown* 6

Tertullian *On Modesty* 4

Cyprian *Epistles* 1.8-9

Novatian *On the Jewish Meats* 3

Arnobius *Against the Heathen* 5.6-7

Arnobius *Against the Heathen* 5.17

Lactantius *The Divine Institutes* 5.9

Constitutions of the Holy Apostles 6.11

Constitutions of the Holy Apostles 6.28

Constitutions of the Holy Apostles 7.2

Origen *Commentary on Matthew* 14.10

9. Nicene and Post-Nicene Fathers

Eusebius *In Praise of Constantine* 13.11

Eusebius *Proof of the Gospel* 4.10

Eusebius *Preparation of the Gospel* 1.4

Eusebius *Theophania* 2.81

Ephraim *Hymns on the Nativity* 1

Basil *Letters* 217.58, 62

Chrysostom *Homilies on Romans* 4

Chrysostom *Homilies on 1 Corinthians* 16

Chrysostom *Homilies on Titus* 5

Augustine *Confessions* 3.8

Augustine *City of God* 16.3

www.ingramcontent.com/pod-product-compliance
Lightning Source LLC
LaVergne TN
LVHW050940080826
845145LV00004B/1339

* 9 7 8 0 9 7 8 5 9 1 7 2 4 *